Augustine, Manichaeism, and the Good

Patristic Studies

Gerald Bray
General Editor

Vol. 2

PETER LANG
New York • Washington, D.C./Baltimore • Boston • Bern
Frankfurt am Main • Berlin • Brussels • Vienna • Canterbury

Kam-lun Edwin Lee

Augustine, Manichaeism, and the Good

PETER LANG
New York • Washington, D.C./Baltimore • Boston • Bern
Frankfurt am Main • Berlin • Brussels • Vienna • Canterbury

Library of Congress Cataloging-in-Publication Data

Lee, Kam-lun Edwin.
Augustine, Manichaeism, and the good / Kam-lun Edwin Lee.
p. cm. — (Patristic studies; vol. 2)
Includes bibliographical references and index.
1. Augustine, Saint, Bishop of Hippo. 2. Manichaeism—Controversial literature—History.
3. Apologetics—History—Early church, ca. 30–600. 4. Good and evil—History.
I. Title. II. Series: Patristic studies (Peter Lang Publishing); vol. 2.
BR65.A9L39   273'.2—dc21   98-30634
ISBN 0-8204-4278-X
ISSN 1094-6217

Die Deutsche Bibliothek-CIP-Einheitsaufnahme

Lee, Kam-lun Edwin:
Augustine, manichaeism, and the good / Kam-lun Edwin Lee.
–New York; Washington, D.C./Baltimore; Boston; Bern;
Frankfurt am Main; Berlin; Brussels; Vienna; Canterbury: Lang.
(Patristic studies; Vol. 2)
ISBN 0-8204-4278-X

The paper in this book meets the guidelines for permanence and durability
of the Committee on Production Guidelines for Book Longevity
of the Council of Library Resources.

Printed in the United States of America

To Pei
my better half

CONTENTS

FOREWORD

Kam-lun Edwin Lee's first achievement in this study is to have dared to explore an area virtually untrodden by scholars until now. For if commentators as far back as Augustine of Hippo's own time have noted the importance his anti-Manichaean polemic placed on denying to evil any substantial reality, their net conclusion was to lavish attention on what evil signified to both Augustine and Manichaeans, with relatively little focus on the notion of the Good, and none at all when it came to Manichaeism. But, as K.E. Lee points out, Manichaean beliefs were constructed upon a radical dichotomy between evil *and good*.

It is the idea of the Good in Manichaeism which K.E. Lee highlights here—not as Manichaeans conceived it, but as Augustine believed they conceived it. The second signal contribution of this book is, therefore, its reference to the Manichaean background for Augustine's own idea of the Good. This is a legitimate objective because the definition he formed of it for himself would have constituted the basis for anything he had to say about the Good (and, for that matter, evil) in Manichaeism. Here it is shown how the Manichaean understanding of the Good (as Augustine understood it) played a role (obviously) in his shaping of the anti-Manichaean polemic, and (less obviously) in developing his own ideas. Beginning with Augustine's earliest work, *De pulchro et apto*, K.E. Lee demonstrates that he understood Manichaeism to equate "goodness" with "beauty" or "tranquil pleasure," an equivalence primarily engaging sensory perception. By extension, the Supreme Good (God) would be that which can guarantee the soul's perpetual tranquil pleasure, and the corollary would identify "evil" with a disturbance of beauty or of the tranquil state.

K.E. Lee also finds in this Manichaean notion of the Good an influence on the development of Augustine's theory of predestination: this was the result of a perceived necessity for an alternative theory of the cosmic order in the face of the Manichaean view of the universe as a mixture of good and evil, one which engaged a radical shift of emphasis from individual self-determination (the primacy of free will) to determination by the divine will.

This book, then, while it does not aim to contribute to the reader's knowledge of Manichaeism, opens several new vistas, relating to impressions Augustine acquired from Manichaeism, and how those impressions helped shape his own thinking in ways more than merely polemical. It should be axiomatic that one cannot know Augustine without knowing Manichaeism, and one hopes that Kam-lun Edwin Lee's study will help make it so.

J. Kevin Coyle
Saint Paul University
Ottawa, Canada

PREFACE

The words that we use most often in our daily language are sometimes hardest to define. The term "good" is one of them. When we say a meal is good, we mean that the dish is delicious, and suiting our taste. A good car would mean that it operates smoothly, and probably with an appealing appearance. But if we call a person good, we usually think in moral terms that he or she does not cheat and is fond of helping others. All the varied adjectival usages of "good" must come back to the basic question of "What is the Good?"

Classical Greek philosophers and Neoplatonists attempted to define *the Good*. To look for the reality behind the changing appearances, Plato thought that the Good is related to being and intelligible form. Aristotle identified the Supreme Good as happiness, but he concluded that no single definition of the Good can be found from which all applications of the term "good" are derivable. Following Plato's line of reasoning, Plotinus equated good with reality and hence taught that evil is only a lack of being. Augustine might be borrowing partly from Aristotle and from Plotinus (and Cicero) on various aspects of the idea of the Good; the main of the idea, however, comes from Manichaean source.

Augustine's thinking is complex. He weaves different sources into a tapestry, unfortunately without the practice of acknowledgment. So, to trace his sources is a recognized challenge. We do not deny the scriptural molding in the Christian Augustine, notably the Pauline view in soteriology. Yet we must also admit other influences some of which are continuous with his pre-conversion days. Much has been done in identifying the Platonic effect; the study of Manichaean contribution, however, is still a virgin land of research. Augustine's early exposure to Manichaeism as an auditor, we can assume, had a life-long effect on him. Therefore, in this study, we will *only* pay attention to the Manichaean thread in Augustine's tapestry to see how it develops, during his formative years prior to 400, in his three notions of Supreme Good, personal evil, and predestination. These belong, respectively, to Augustine's doctrine of God, of sin, and of salvation.

Regarding Manichaean influence on Augustine, we may wonder whether it is a result of conscious effort on his part. Augustine is a master polemist fond of employing the opponents' category in order to make his arguments understandable to the other party, and ultimately to defeat them on their own ground. The use of Manichaean categories therefore belongs to his conscious effort of adaptation, always with fresh content. During the adaptation process, however, his developing idea is sometimes unwittingly limited to a certain perspective, which may color even his scriptural interpretation. As it will be shown in this book, Augustine's version of predestination is more than pure biblical exegesis, although he can find supporting prooftexts for his view. His understanding of predestination in terms of divine secret election is intimately linked to his *Manichaean* idea of the Good as the Beautiful. Thus, beyond contributing to patristic studies in tracing the Manichaean influence in Augustine, this work has systematic theological implications. Put in historical context, Augustine's doctrine of predestination (and hence, soteriology) is not merely a distillation of Pauline theology that must be regarded as gospel truth. As argued in the conclusion, the strong determinism (lacking in the teachings of Ambrose and other contemporary Church fathers) in Augustine's mature view of grace emerges out of his struggle with the Manichaean view of the cosmos in the process of his adaptation of the idea of the Good. In the past, St. Augustine's theology has almost been held sacrosanct in Christian orthodoxy. This historical study makes way for a less absolute understanding of Augustine, however important he has been in the Western Church tradition; it leaves room for re-interpretation of Paul's teaching on election in a less deterministic manner. This loosening from the bind of Augustinian dogmatics is beneficial to contextual theological thinking where the controlling ideas—like Augustine's doctrine of predestination—in the Western tradition must be reevaluated in light of *exegesis* and an accurate understanding of the historico-cultural conditioning behind Western theology.

A word is in order concerning how this book should be read. Since this work is an adaptation of my doctoral dissertation on patristic studies, the chapters are organized to prove a thesis, namely, that there is Manichaean influence in Augustine's view of the Good. The introduction deals with methodology. Chapter one supplies the background on Augustine's relation with Manichaeism, but the content of the Manichaean myth will not be mentioned until chapter five under the section of **A Response to Manichaeism**. Chapter two is the most technical yet foundational in establishing the thesis by showing that Augustine understands the Manichaean idea of the Good as the Beautiful. Nonetheless, Augustine disagrees with the Manichees' materialistic interpretation of what true beauty is. Chapters three to five document Augustine's Christian adaptation of the Manichaean idea of the Good to his notions of Supreme Good, personal evil, and predestination. The conclusion summarizes the results and draws out the implications. Read chapter two last if it is found too dry.

The completion of this study owes to many but only a few can be mentioned here. I must thank the late Professor Klaus Bockmühl of Regent College, Vancouver, B.C., who has served as my role model in theological formation. His constant advice to students is "major author, major theme." Also, thanks must be rendered to Professor J. Kevin Coyle of St. Paul University, Ottawa, who supervised my Ph.D. dissertation with personable and knowledgeable guidance. The excellent resources at St. Paul University library and the generous help of its staff lightened my task. The loving support and encouragement of my wife Pei was indispensable, especially during dark hours. I should thank Dr. Timothy Yates and Rev. Rick Cook for their help in reading the manuscript and making valuable suggestions. The funding of this publication is a love gift from relatives and friends of the Chinese Christian communities in Canada to which I belong.

Kam-lun Edwin Lee
China Ministries International
Taipei, Taiwan

ABBREVIATIONS

Augustine's Works

Collection of Text

AB   Abulesz, Peter. "*S. Aurelii Augustini: De Genesi contra Manichaeos Libri duo, De Octo Quaestionibus ex Veteri Testamento.*" Ph.D. diss., Universität Wien, 1972.
CC   *Corpus Christianorum, Series Latina.*
CSEL   *Corpus Scriptorum Ecclesiasticorum Latinorum.*
PL   Migne, Jacques-Paul. *Patrologiae Cursus Completus, Series Latina.*

Individual Works Used in the Study (*in Chronological Order*)

pul. apt.   *De pulchro et apto* (*On Beauty and Suitability*) (380)
Acad.   *Contra Academicos* (*Against the Academics*) (386)
beat. uit.   *De beata uita* (*On Happy Life*) (386)
ord.   *De ordine* (*On Order*) (386)
epis.   *Epistulae* (*Epistles*) (386–429)
mor. I & II *De moribus ecclesiae Catholicae et de moribus Manichaeorum* (*On the Morals of the Catholic Church and On the Morals of the Manichees*) (387/388–389)
Gen. Man.   *De Genesi contra Manichaeos* (*On Genesis Against the Manichees*) (388)
lib. arb.   *De libero arbitrio* (*On the Free Choice of the Will*) (388–394/395)
diu. quaes. *De diuersis quaestionibus 83* (*Responses to Various Questions*) (388–395/396)
mus.   *De musica* (*On Music*) (388/390)
uer. rel.   *De uera religione* (*On True Religion*) (390)
util.   *De utilitate credendi* (*On the Usefulness of Believing*) (391/392)

duab. anim.	*De duabus animabus* (*On the Two Souls*) (391/392)
serm.	*Sermones* (*Sermons*) (391–428)
Fort.	*Contra Fortunatum* (*Against Fortunatus*) (392)
fid. sym.	*De fide et symbolo* (*On Faith and the Creed*) (393)
ser. dom.	*De sermone domini in monte* (*On the Sermon on the Mount*) (393/394–395)
Adim.	*Contra Adimantum* (*Against Adimantus*) (393/394)
exp. Rom.	*Expositio quarumdam propositionum ex Epistula ad Romanos* (*Expositions of 84 Propositions Concerning the Epistles to the Romans*) (394)
Simpl.	*Ad Simplicianum* (*To Simplician*) (396)
fund.	*Contra epistulam fundamenti* (*Against the Epistle of the Fundamentals*) (396)
ago.	*De agone christiano* (*The Christian Struggle*) (396)
doc. chr.	*De doctrina christiana* (*On Christian Instruction*) (396/397–426/427)
ennar.	*Ennarationes in Psalmos* (*Expositions on Psalms*) (396–416)
conf.	*Confessiones* (*Confessions*) (397–400)
Faus.	*Contra Faustum* (*Against Faustus*) (397–398/399)
Fel.	*Acta habita cum Felice* (*Proceedings of Debate with Felix*) (398)
nat. bon.	*De natura boni* (*On the Nature of the Good*) (399)
Secun.	*Contra epistulam Secundini* (*Against the Epistle of Secundinus*) (399)
trin.	*De trinitate* (*On the Trinity*) (400–421)
ciu.	*De ciuitate dei* (*The City of God*) (411–426)
Iul.	*Contra Iulianum* (*Against Julian*) (422)
retr.	*Retractationes* (*Retractions*) (427)
haer.	*De haeresibus* (*On Heresies*) (ca. 428)

Other Work

Enn.	MacKenna, Stephen, trans. *Plotinus: The Enneads*. 2nd ed. Revised by B.S. Page. London: Faber and Faber, 1956.

INTRODUCTION

Why choose St. Augustine, Bishop of Hippo, as a research subject? Well-meaning friends advised me against the choice for fear that I might not succeed in the research. The advice is genuine because they have either heard horror stories or seen others fail. Or they themselves have once attempted a similar task but eventually decided to change direction. Yet, I doubted whether these were good enough reasons to avoid Augustine. If it is only difficult, but not impossible, to write on Augustine, then I want to know if I can do it, by God's grace. I chose to study St. Augustine because he has had incalculable influence on the whole Western Church tradition, Catholic and Protestant alike. In today's Asian theological milieu, the demand to think contextually at the same time must call for reevaluation of the Western tradition, and Augustine is a good starting point. My personal curiosity about predestination further motivated me to investigate Augustine's notion of the Good because the appreciation of the former is conditional upon the understanding of the latter.

Augustine of Hippo's notion of the Good is an important topic of study in its own right. To date, studies have been done on various aspects of Augustine's view of the Good, such as its Platonic roots,[1] the nature of created good,[2] human goodness,[3] goodness as order,[4] the issue of theodicy,[5] and that of predestination in the context of divine goodness.[6] Yet, so far no work has been done on the Manichaean influence upon his concept of the Good.[7] Even on other topics, the study of a possible Manichaean influence on Augustine is still at an early stage.[8] It is well-known that Augustine's earliest controversy with the Manichees contributed significantly to the development of his thought throughout his life. Johannes Van Oort, one of the leading scholars on Augustinian and Manichaean studies, remarks that it will be difficult to understand Augustine's theology without a background knowledge of Manichaeism.[9] The study of a possible Manichaean influence on Augustine's notion of the Good is particularly pertinent because Manichaeism is at heart a dualistic solution to the problem of good and evil.

So far, the most substantial treatments of Augustine's notion of the Good from the viewpoint of his Manichaean background are G.R. Evan's *Augustine on Evil* and G. Sfameni Gasparro's survey on the nature and origin of evil.[10] But, from the consideration of Manichaean influence, the concept of evil is not exactly the same as the mere opposite of what is good. While Evan addresses a more general issue, this study tries to determine specifically how Augustine's understanding of the Manichaean idea of the Good influences his own related notions concerning that same theme. We assume here that Manichaeism as seen through the eyes of Augustine would be different from the Manichaeism with which he came into contact. Our focus on the former is reasonable because it is Augustine's own understanding which directly contributes to the development of his thinking. Hence, there will be no treatment here of the notion of the Good in Manichaeism *per se*, nor any discussion of the objectivity of Augustine's reports on his former religion.[11]

Our investigation will employ the historical-critical method, which seeks to unravel the true meaning of a text by examining its inner consistency and by putting the text within a larger context (in this case, Augustine's corpus), those traditions on which it drew, and the circumstances under which it appeared. We will use critical editions of Augustine's works where available. For texts unavailable in a truly critical edition, we will resort to Jacques-Paul Migne's *Patrologiae Cursus Completus, Series Latina*.

This research proceeds in two stages: the establishment of Augustine's understanding of the Manichaean notion of the Good throughout our period of inquiry; and the study of how this understanding influenced his related ideas. The first stage consists of showing what Augustine understands by the Manichaean notion of the Good in *De natura boni* (399),[12] his last formal anti-Manichaean treatise, as well as in *De pulchro et apto* (380), his earliest writing. In the process, the issues of dating and occasion of composition of *De natura boni* are examined, and the content and motive of writing of *De pulchro et apto* are explored. The second stage entails the investigation of the continuous influence of the notion of the Good, in the writings between 380 and 399 (also included is *Confessiones* XIII, written in 400). This is done in two senses: 1) Augustine's choice of approach, despite the use of a Neoplatonic vehicle, to the treatment of God as the Supreme Good and to the problem of evil, and 2) his development of the notion of predestination, already in place with *Ad Simplicianum* (396).

In the investigation of the contributing Manichaean influences on Augustine's idea of Supreme Good, we attempt, first, to identify the place of "supreme measure" in both his earliest and latest anti-Manichaean treatises; second, to trace how this idea developed in *De beata uita* as an answer to his consideration of the happy life in *De pulchro et apto*; and third, to show that the same idea also acquires a creational aspect.

In studying how Augustine's grasp of the Manichaean concept of the Good affects his notion of evil, we investigate the Manichaean concept of evil—again, as Augustine understood it. Here, we will see how Augustine retains the Manichaean insight regarding the upset state of the subjective disposition, yet replaces the ontological explication of evil by the concept of the flesh. He develops this concept in the notions of *consuetudo* (or "habit") and concupiscence.

On the idea of predestination, Augustine's mature notion in *Ad Simplicianum* means that God's gracious but hidden election predetermines the salvation or condemnation of each person. While some are left alone, God's prevenient grace prepares for the faith of the elect to respond favorably to the divine calling. In this context, we can identify two fundamental issues: the hiddenness of God's gracious election and the inevitability of personal evil. Here, we will show two aspects of influence from the Manichaean notion of the Good. First, in Augustine's consideration of cosmic order as beautiful, he really tries to address the Manichaean view concerning things in the universe: that which is beautiful is good. Second, Augustine's maturation of the concept of personal evil, which will have been shown to be of Manichaean influence, forces a change in his conceptual framework of the cosmic order that is reflective of the notion of hiddenness of divine election. But this is not all. Manichaeism also contributes to Augustine's doctrine of predestination by way of its foundational context in both eschatological and cosmic aspects. This context is developed out of Augustine's idea of Supreme Good—a result of Manichaean influence.

CHAPTER ONE

AUGUSTINE AND MANICHAEISM

Augustine's Manichaean Years

Although Augustine was never fully initiated into Manichaeism,[1] he is credited by scholars with knowing it reasonably well.[2] Possibly still keeping some ties with the Catholic Church,[3] Augustine for nine years[4] was a Manichaean auditor.[5] It is, therefore, no surprise that he appears to have had comprehensive knowledge of Manichaean doctrines, at least in their Roman African form. Though Augustine in his polemics cites only two writings of Mani by name, *Epistula Fundamenti* and *Thesaurus* (e.g., *nat. bon.* xliv),[6] it is obvious that he knew of more. He knew many of the Manichaean works in existence at that time (*conf.* III.vi.10; *Faus.* XIII.6; *fund.* xxviii), and he seems to have made the reading of Mani's own writings a personal goal.[7] Prior to his first encounter with Faustus, a well-known speaker on evangelistic discourse and a debater in the Manichaean sect whose reputation went well beyond the bounds of North Africa,[8] Augustine had been studying Mani's writings with zeal (*conf.* V.vii.13) and he took care to compare Mani's pronouncements regarding astrology with the teachings of the philosophers on the subject of astronomical manifestations (*conf.* V.iii.3, 6). To the heaven-oriented Augustine, astrology is the testing ground for the validity of Manichaeism. His fascination with the former might, in the first place, have drawn him toward the latter, which regards the heavenly bodies as the dwelling place of divine beings.[9] The reason for his break with Manichaeism was Faustus' inability "to vanquish the astronomers and vindicate the Manichaean worship of Sun and Moon."[10] Despite his fame as a well-known speaker in matters of evangelistic discourse, it seems evident in the debate with Augustine that Faustus might not have been effective at inter-faith dialogues.[11] The very fact that the heavenly bodies revered by the Manichees were subject to calculations and predictions by the philosophers must have made Augustine think twice about the divine nature of the beings dwelling in these bodies. It has been convincingly argued that Augustine's decision to break with the Manichees was precipitated by the accuracy of astronomical predictions of two solar eclipses during his Manichaean years between 372/373 and 383 (the year when Faustus went to Carthage).[12] Nevertheless, Augustine's break with Manichaeism seems also to have been due to the ever-increasing problems he found with the sect in terms of the inherent contradictions within their professed faith—especially the Manichaean belief that God can be harmed by evil (e.g., *mor.* II.xii.25)—which possibly was the motive behind his early desire to meet with Faustus.[13] Eventually, after his encounter with Faustus, an occasion he expected to solve all his doubts, Augustine decided to detach himself from the sect (*conf.* V.vii.13). His wide exposure to general literature enabled him to judge right away that Faustus had not read beyond those works of his own sect which were in Latin (*conf.* V.vi.11). Due to his knowledge of Manichaean doctrines, Augustine was able to see through the problems inherent in the system. Subsequently, he conscientiously attempted to steer clear of these problems as he adapted the Manichaean notion of the Good.

Certainly, Augustine was not the only Christian thinker writing against Manichaeism in his time, and so it is very possible that his ideas are not all original. But Augustine did have a privileged position among other anti-Manichaean polemists by the fact that he alone had belonged to the Manichees.[14] Also, there is evidence that he relies partly on Plotinus in his attack, although Plotinus did not write against Manichaeism but Gnosticism. Augustine's general familiarity with Platonic ideas, which he applies to his anti-Manichaean refutation, may be shown by the similarity in style, and sometimes even in content, between the anti-Manichaean treatise of the Middle Platonist Alexander of Lycopolis and the anti-Manichaean writings of Augustine himself.

Manichaeism of Roman Africa

The Roman African branch of Manichaeism is recognized by some scholars as having characteristics that distinguish it from Manichaeism in other places. L.H. Grondijs cautions that due to the extreme adaptability of Manichaeism to its environment, each sect had its own unique content of belief. He traces the sources (current Christian and philosophical ideas) which the North African Manichees could have drawn upon to shape their faith.[15] Disagreeing with Grondijs' emphasis on the particularity of North African Manichaeism, Decret argues that this branch has no essential difference from the one in Rome concerning doctrines and practices.[16] Thus, it is more correct to speak of "Roman and African Manichaeism."

The uniqueness of Roman African Manichaeism is believed to be shaped by both the religious milieu and the political context of the Roman world. L.J.R. Ort observes this: the Western Manichees tended to ignore Mani's Babylonian origin.[17] The desire to be perceived as a part of Christianity definitely motivated the Roman African Manichees to adopt some Christian elements into their belief. For one, they held the Apostle Paul and his writings in high regard.[18] There was also a political motivation. In order to avoid persecution, the Manichees would at times disguise themselves as Christians.[19] It is also believed that the Western Manichees maintained a relative silence about Mani's country of origin because they would have been perceived as anti-Roman if they proclaimed a foreigner from Persia as their religious leader.[20]

Reason for Anti-Manichaean Campaign

Because Roman African Manichaeism adapts easily to the Christian environment, it was considered a real threat to the Catholic Church. Simple Christians had a good chance of being taken in by the Christian appearance of this branch of Manichaeism (*Gen. Man.* I.i.2). Someone like Augustine's friend Romanianus who lacked a good grounding in the faith could become easy prey (*uer. rel.* vii.12). Romanianus may well have been highly educated,[21] yet Augustine was concerned with the less learned who, without the intellectual ability to appreciate the invisible spiritual reality,[22] might accept the Manichaean arguments against the Old Testament. Without able and willing Christian teachers to counter the Manichaean doctrines, inexperienced Catholics might easily be led astray (*mor.* I.i.1–2). Augustine obliquely puts this critical situation in a positive light: the heretics have, by divine providence, done good to the Church by provoking carnal Catholics to seek the truth and, at the same time, spiritual Catholics to expound it (*uer. rel.* viii.15; cf. *Gen. Man.* I.i.2). Why such a shortage of qualified teachers? Augustine explains that many who were able teachers were afraid of drawing too much unnecessary publicity (*util.* ii.4). Consequently, he was forced to do it himself.[23] His mission statement is well summarized in his recital of the advice of his Christian friends: "to expel those ruinous errors from the minds of even the inexperienced."[24]

On the other hand, Augustine also aimed at converting soft Manichees or Manichaean sympathizers, some of whom stayed in Manichaeism for the lack of a better alternative.[25] In this group of people, a few were known to Augustine—former friends from his youth (*duab. anim.* xiv.23–xv.24) and friends like Honoratus whom he had helped convert to Manichaeism (*util.* i.2). Augustine confesses that Honoratus' well-being, not that of others, is his concern (*util.* i.3). It seems possible that, besides desiring to be truthful with his friends (*util.* ii.4; cf. *duab. anim.* xv.24), Augustine might have judged that personal relationships could assist his effort of winning them over to Christianity. He did not hesitate to speak of his own weaknesses in being susceptible to the lure of Manichaeism and of his struggle in finding the true faith in the Catholic Church (*util.* i.2). He regretted that he had left the faith implanted in him during his boyhood, for otherwise he could have helped his friends even earlier, though it still might not be too late to make amends (*duab. anim.* i.1; xv.24).

Even to those Manichees like Secundinus or their professed sympathizers who were showing openness to genuine conversation, Augustine would try to speak at their level in the hope of winning them over. Hence, he would rather start with reasoning instead of the Catholic authority (*mor.* I.ii.3). Addressing them with gentleness and understanding (*Secun.* i; *fund.* ii, iii), Augustine wanted to create room for honest exchange (*fund.* iii), hoping that he could dissuade them from Manichaeism (*fund.* xliii) and even invite them to conversion (*Secun.* xxvi; *mor.* I.xxxv.77; II.xvi.51). Harsh words, however, were reserved for the unyielding (*Faus.* XXXIII.6). Augustine claims to have conducted himself in good faith in every possible way (cf. *Gen. Man.* II.xxix.43) in order to heal, not to destroy, one who strays (*fund.* i; *mor.* I.i.2). His agenda is clear. His primary concern is not to convert the obstinate, but to stem the tide of Manichaeism which was damaging the Catholic Church. That explains why he exhorts the Manichees to stop attacking the Church and desist from misleading weaker Catholics (*mor.* I.xxxv.80).

With this agenda of Augustine in mind, we may be able to put his debates with Fortunatus and Felix into perspective. His purpose is to discredit Manichaeism before interested audiences, so that they may be strengthened in faith or, at least, better disposed toward Christianity. In this respect, Augustine was successful when he cornered Fortunatus in debate, so that the latter fell just short of admitting an official defeat (*Fort.* 36). Fortunatus then left Hippo (*retr.* I.xv.1). To judge from their reaction at the end of the first debate session, we can see that Fortunatus' position on Scripture did not at all endear him to the audience (*Fort.* 19). As for Felix, he was forced by argument, as well as administrative pressure, into signing a statement anathematizing Manichaeism. By the time the debate with Felix took place, Manichaeism had not only been outlawed but was also overtly suppressed by the government. Under such circumstances, Felix was hardly treated as Augustine's equal. Prior to the debate, Felix's books were confiscated by the authorities, and between the two debate sessions he was put under surveillance.[26] Although it is doubtful whether Felix truly rejected Manichaeism by signing the statement,[27] the effect on the audience was obviously favorable (*Fel.* II.xxii). It may not be easy to evaluate the effects of Augustine's attack on the spread of Manichaeism in North Africa after his time, for lack of information,[28] yet we know that the tide was gradually stemmed. Toward the end of the anti-Manichaean controversy, Augustine prayed: "Grant that through our ministry, whereby you have willed that this cursed and most horrible error be refuted, others be liberated just as many have already been liberated."[29] But what did Augustine think of as the most fundamental issue hindering the Manichees from arriving at the truth?

Critique of Manichaean Epistemology

Commenting on the physical or materialistic nature of the Manichaean religious language, Jason David BeDuhn warns us against assigning it too easily to the metaphorical category. For the Manichees, as he observes, the perception of reality is based on their physical practices. Thus, BeDuhn remarks:

> By conceptually grounding their daily behaviour in the fundamental structures of the universe, Manichaeans collapsed physics into metaphysics, physiology into cosmology, and dietetics into sacrality. At the same time, they apprehended the entire universe in all its many dimensions in the light of the regimen by which they lived. It was through this regimen, this code of relations, that the Manichaeans sought to control the universe in which they found themselves, and attempted to rectify the problematic givenness of their existence.[30]

Augustine seems to understand this point well and directs his critique accordingly. He believes that what leads the Manichees to arrive at a dualistic ontology is their problematic epistemology of vulgar materialism. They are deceived by material images because they rely on the senses for their judgment: the beauty of color, the sweetness of taste, the fragrance of smell (*mor.* II.xvi.38–40, 43).[31] Nevertheless, this does not mean that the Manichees are satisfied with what they sense in the physical world. Augustine probably understands that the Manichaean rejection of the Old Testament portrayal of God is in fact a move to transcend the purely physical (cf. *conf.* III.vii.12).

Augustine judges that the Manichees think dualistically according to what they like or dislike, which accordingly they assign to good and evil natures respectively (*uer. rel.* ix.16; *Faus.* XXXII.20; *Gen. Man.* I.xiii.19).[32] He further charges that the Manichees can find an evil principle alongside the good principle because they look too much for the source of evil (*util.* xviii.36),[33] and consequently mistake the substance that is sinfully loved as substantial evil (*uer. rel.* xx.38). The Manichees, as Augustine sees it, are making an objective substance out of subjective feeling.

Yet, Augustine believes that even when Manichees recoil from the senses, they carry with them the impressions and images received from the senses (*util.* i.1). This projected imagination from objects of the senses is what he calls "phantasms." They can be divided, multiplied, contracted, expanded, set in order, disturbed, or given any shape in the consciousness (*memoria*)[34] In the search for truth, such confusing images are hard to ward off (*uer. rel.* x.18; *fund.* ii, iii). For the Manichees to understand truth is nothing other than to think of corporeal forms, whether finite or infinite (*Faus.* XX.7). Since phantasms spring from spatial and temporal things (*uer. rel.* xxxix.73) just as light has extension in space and in time (*uer. rel.* xlix.97), so the God conceived of in this way is also extended in space and time (*mor.* I.x.17; *fund.* xviii, xxiii).[35] Hence, Augustine charges the Manichees with a view that God has to go from one place to another and that the divine substance is able to escape from entrapment (*mor.* II.xvi.43),[36] and therefore they ask "When did God create the universe?" (*Gen. Man.* I.ii.3,4).[37] The best the Manichees can do is to infinitely extend what they see (*uer. rel.* xx.40).[38] So, the divine substance is extended through infinite space but needs to be cut short on one side to make room for evil (*fund.* xlii–xliii).

In spite of the fact that the Manichaean perception of reality is more than can be met with the senses, Augustine never thought that the Manichees had the insight really to go beyond the material form of things to their true reality,[39] since simple images cannot satisfy the desire of the seeker of truth (*conf.* III.vi.10).[40] Actually, Augustine believed that when the Manichees worship their phantasms, they are committing idolatry (*conf.* IV.ii.3) of a kind worse than that of the pagans who at least worship true objects (*Faus.* XX.5; cf. *conf.* III.vi.10). Despite their moral asceticism,[41] their lack of intellectual penetration shuts them out from the truth (*uer. rel.* liv.104–106; xvi.30). The ability to penetrate is spiritual in nature[42] (*Gen. Man.* II.xxv.38) and is God's gift (*uer. rel.* 105) for the purpose of discerning spiritual things (*duab. anim.* ix.2).[43] Without this ability, the Manichees find fault with the Old Testament which teaches deep spiritual things in figurative terms (*mor.* I.xvii.30, xx.37).

In the imaginary world of "the beyond," the Manichees believe that God and the soul are of the same divine substance. The Manichaean argument for consubstantiality is that since the soul is good and God is the source of good, soul must come from God. But the relation between source and product is substantial. Augustine would agree with this line of reasoning except that the relation is not substantial, but one of divine freedom as an outflow of divine goodness (*Fort.* 11–13; *Fel.* II.xxi). Augustine blames the Manichees' theory of substantial relation between God and the soul on their vulgar materialistic outlook. Perhaps he thinks that they are "materialistic" not only in the narrow sense as projecting the notion of the visible body to the invisible extended form (an aspect of their dualism), but also in the wider sense of positing consubstantiality between God and the soul.

Augustine accuses the Manichees of having a vulgar materialistic outlook. His accusation is an indictment of their inductive approach from the visible to the invisible. Augustine thinks that, with such an approach, their resultant ontology is not well thought out. By contrast, when Augustine formulates his own alternative, he starts with an ontological supposition of theistic monism, which comes mainly from the teaching of the Catholic Church, with help from Neoplatonism.[44] This change of starting point leads Augustine to ask a different opening question in his investigation. Instead of asking, "Where does evil come from?" (*Unde sit malum?*), he prefers to ask, "What is evil?" (*Quid sit malum?*) (*mor.* II.ii.2).[45] From his starting point of Neoplatonically informed theistic monism, the concept of the nature of the Good may be defined from the perspective of being or existence. Augustine's claim to a more spiritual outlook really means his deductive methodology, one which presupposes a form of revealed truth taught by the Catholic Church. Having said that, we do not mean that Augustine borrows nothing from the Manichees regarding the notion of the Good. In the following two chapters, we will show that his ideas of Supreme Good and of evil are inspired by the Manichaean notion of the Good.[46] But first we need to find out his understanding of this notion.

CHAPTER TWO

MANICHAEAN IDEA OF THE GOOD

In *De Natura Boni*

Among Augustine's anti-Manichaean writings, *De natura boni* is the only treatise that deals explicitly with the theme of the nature of the Good, although the theme is also broached in other works. It is therefore reasonable to expect that if he has anything to say about the Manichaean notion of the Good, it should be found here.

Dating of the Treatise

In *Retractationes* II.ix, Augustine tells us neither the date nor the occasion of composition. A. Anthony Moon relates that the traditional dating of 404 has been severely disputed by Paul Monceaux and his follower Seraphinus Zarb who favor the earlier date of 399.[1] The whole matter depends on the dating of the preceding work, *Acta habita cum Felice*, which is traditionally dated at 404. We now address this latter issue.

Whether we accept Monceaux's dating, the chronological discrepancy in *retr.* II.ix around the writing of *Acta habita cum Felice* (assuming the traditional dating) cannot be denied.[2] *Contra litteras Petiliani*, dated between 400 and 403, is put in sixteenth place after *Acta habita cum Felice*. To explain this phenomenon, Monceaux assumes that the copyist mistook VI for IV in regard to the consulship mentioned in *Fel.* I.i, and hence scholars traditionally assign 404, instead of 398, as the date for the debate with Felix.[3] This proposal has met serious challenge from Decret on two fronts. Decret attempts to show that the copyist's mistake is unlikely, and that the match between calendar calculation and internal data points to the 404 dating.[4] While the first part is still an argument of likelihood, the second part aims at a definitive defeat of Monceaux's theory. Decret follows the observation of Le Nain de Tillemont who noted that the seventh day of December when the debate with Felix first took place was a Wednesday (*Fel.* I.i).[5] The reasoning is that the resumption of the second meeting of the debate was a Monday (*Fel.* I.xx), which was mentioned by Augustine as the fifth day after their first meeting (*post diem [...] quintum*) (*Fel.* II.i). By backdating five days, one may easily conclude that the first debate occurred on the previous Wednesday. And according to Decret's calculation, the seventh of December of 404 is indeed Wednesday (whereas, by deduction, the same day in 398 would have been a Tuesday). The traditional dating appears vindicated. Nevertheless, careful calculation reveals Decret's error in identification. The seventh of December in 404 was in fact a Thursday, whereas that same day in 398 was a Wednesday. Instead of defeating Monceaux's theory, the observation of Le Nain de Tillemont helps definitively confirm it. Hence, *De natura boni* can be reasonably dated to 399. This is consistent with the following study.

Occasion of Writing

Based on the maturity of the work as well as its position as the last of the Bishop of Hippo's formal anti-Manichaean treatises, Moon fairly assesses the work as Augustine's epitome, and even a handbook, of anti-Manichaean polemic.[6] Having said that, Moon has not yet explained why the theme of "the nature of the Good" should become the issue for systematic treatment at this final stage. In other words, we must ask whether the composition of *De natura boni* is an isolated incident of systematization and why "the nature of the Good" becomes the explicitly dominant theme at this point.

Development of systematic treatment.   As an effort of systematization, *De natura boni* stands in the middle of Augustine's development of a methodical polemic against Manichaeism. This development begins with *Contra epistulam fundamenti* (396). Recognizing that the *Epistle of the Foundation* contains almost all of the Manichaean belief (*fund.* v) and is very possibly a handbook for Manichaean catechumens,[7] Augustine obviously wants to decisively refute Manichaeism.[8] This differs from his earlier efforts of simply uncovering the deceptive tricks the Manichees use to win people over (*mor.* I.i.2) or of focusing on a single issue of Manichaean doctrine, such as that of human inner struggle (*duab. anim.* i.1).

Moreover, when Moon points out that *De natura boni* is Augustine's last formal anti-Manichaean treatise,[9] we should not overlook that it still precedes the last book of *Confessiones* (400),[10] whose composition must be considered from the perspective of the anti-Manichaean motive. *Conf.* XIII, though not strictly a systematic work or a treatise, is a positive synthetic exposition of "the Good" in the context of creation and re-creation. To reject the notions of an impotent God and of dualism in Manichaeism (xxx.45), Augustine affirms the self-sufficient and omnipotent goodness of God who is the sole supreme reality in the universe to bring good by forming the creation and re-forming fallen humankind (i.1, ii.2–3, iv.5). Viewed from this angle, the writing of *De natura boni* is not an isolated incident. As a summary statement, it bridges the gap between the foregoing polemics and the grand synthesis in *conf.* XIII.

Emerging emphasis on the nature of the Good.   But why did Augustine choose to write on the nature of the Good at this time? This may be answered by looking into the role of the debates with Faustus and Felix and the literary form of *De natura boni*. To understand what Augustine has in mind when addressing the theme of the nature of the Good, we may study the opening statements of *De natura boni* (i–ii), which are summarized in *retr.* II.ix:

> The book *On the Nature of the Good* is against the Manichees. There it is shown that God is immutable by nature and is the Supreme Good, and that other natures whether spiritual or corporeal are from him, as well as that, inasmuch as they are natures, they are good. Also [it is shown] what or whence evil is, what great evils the Manichees assign to a good nature and what great good things they attribute to an evil nature, the natures their own error has fabricated.[11]

Three points are mentioned here: 1) God as the Supreme Good is unchangeable, 2) God's nature is different from creation, and 3) dualism is an error. Therefore, by addressing the nature of the Good, Augustine wants to affirm God's inviolability and his non-consubstantiality with creation. His concern regarding these issues had already appeared very early as part of his objection against Manichaeism (e.g., *mor.* II.xi.21). But as he approaches the later part of the anti-Manichaean controversy, they become more clearly a rallying point. Hence, in his encounter with Fortunatus (392), Augustine begins the debate by condemning the Manichaean implication of God's violability as the biggest mistake (*Fort.* 1). Against Faustus and Felix, he puts these objections in summary form. Thus, he protests to Faustus:

> Your fable is long and useless. It is childish play, amusement for women, an old wives' tale containing a broken beginning, a rotten middle and an end that collapses. If you begin by saying that God is immortal, invisible, incorruptible, then what harm could the race of darkness do to him if he refuses to fight with them? And as regards the middle, in what way is God incorruptible and uncontaminable whose members in fruits and vegetables are purified by your eating and digesting? And as to the end, what has the miserable soul done to deserve the punishment of perpetual confinement in the mass of darkness, a punishment which is not due to its own sin but to that of another—the God who due to his deficiency has not been able to cleanse the defilement of the soul that is sent by him to be polluted?[12]

In short, Augustine thinks that God, according to the Manichaean theory, is violable, for otherwise God would not need even to defend himself from the onslaught of the race of darkness. Moreover, to teach that God's members are mixed with fruits and vegetables is to assert consubstantiality between God and creation. Lastly, to affirm that God sends the soul to be mixed with the mass of darkness for his sake but punishes the soul is to make God unjust. Similar points are reiterated when Felix challenges Augustine to show him the falsity of the Manichaean belief:

> Far be it from the hearts which search or hold the truth that they should believe that God, forced by necessity, plunged his substance into that of demons to be bound and polluted. Far be it from the faithful to believe that God, in order to liberate his substance, converts himself into males against females and into females against males to excite their concupiscence. Far be it from the faithful to believe that God himself plunged his substance into the demons and then eternally damned it.[13]

Again, Augustine's first and third objections regarding the violability and the injustice of God are unmistakable. The second point about liberating divine substance by means of sexual intercourse seems to be radically different from that of mastication. Nonetheless, both refer to ways of delivering light particles from the commixture. As such, Augustine is criticizing the Manichaean notion of consubstantiality.

Having shown that the governing themes of divine inviolability and non-consubstantiality in *De natura boni* are already Augustine's central concern in the two debates, we must not overlook the fact that even the third charge receives substantial coverage in the treatise under the theme of penalty for sinners, a derived notion of evil (xxxi–xl; cf. xi, xx). Thus, since sinning is the sinner's voluntary turning away from God, he or she is morally responsible. Contrary to the Manichaean teaching that God is responsible for the soul's sinning, God is just to penalize sinners.

Viewed in light of the two debates, therefore, *De natura boni* may be understood as a positive statement to address what is summarily critiqued in debate with Faustus and Felix. This leads to the question about the literary form used in the treatise, or, to put it differently: Why instead of a sequel to *Contra epistulam fundamenti* Augustine produced *De natura boni*? This becomes a point of interest since he has announced in the former treatise the intention to continue to refute the *Epistle of the Foundation* (*fund.* xliii). In *retr.* II.ii, we are told that he in fact has everything in note form, just waiting for the "leisure," which he never found, to put together a complete point-by-point rebuttal of the fundamentals of the Manichaean belief.[14] Obviously, by choosing to write *De natura boni* instead at this time, Augustine must have thought that the new treatise served a better purpose to counter Manichaeism under the new circumstances. The only major intervening events between 397 and 399 which could have changed his mind are the debates with Faustus (397–398) and Felix (398). As we have shown, Augustine's central objections to Manichaeism at that time contributed directly to the positive content of *De natura boni*.

If content is the only matter of concern, Augustine might indeed be tempted to simply complete his sequel, since he has already substantially treated the theme of the nature of the Good in the latter part of *Contra epistulam fundamenti*. But as a positive statement, the literary form of a rebuttal—in which the discussion will be governed by the Manichaean text—cannot serve the purpose of thematization. Augustine must now recast his material, whether already in prose form as part of the text of the existing work or in note form for the preparation of its sequel, into a new mold. This hypothesis can explain two phenomena: 1) the material on the theme of the nature of the Good in the later portion of *Contra epistulam fundamenti* is reused in the first third of *De natura boni* (i–xxiii), and 2) the critique of the *Epistula Fundamenti* continues in the last third of the latter from where it left off in the former.

To prove the first point, we compare the following sections of *Contra epistulam fundamenti* and *De natura boni* to observe the rearrangement:

nat. bon.		*fund.*
i.	God as the unchangeable Supreme Good creation not of the same nature as God	xxxvii
ii	Manichaean problem of judgment of evil	cf. xxxii

iii–vi	measure, form and order as good in creation and evil the corruption of these goods	xxxviii–xl
vii	cleaving to God's incorruptible beauty	xlii
viii	beauty of temporal order in speech	xli
ix–xi	corruption as judgment permitted by God is part of the just order	xli
xii–xiii	absurdity of Manichaean attribution to what is good and what is evil	xxix–xxxi
xiv–xxiii	nature is good, only corruption of nature is evil	xxxiii–xxxv

From the above comparison, we may conclude that the parallel is no mere coincidence. More, we observe that the lengthy anti-Manichaean polemic in *fund.* xxix–xxxv is placed after the positive assertions on the theme of the Good.

To prove the second point, we note that the starting point of the critique of the Manichaean myth[15] in *De natura boni* (xli) is a summary of the last point of the same critique in *Contra epistulam fundamenti* (xxx; cf. xxxiii): the inhabitants in the region of darkness are said to have vitality, potency, intelligence, but particularly harmony of bodily parts. Furthermore, immediately in the next paragraph of *De natura boni* (xlii), Augustine explicitly resumes his critique of the *Epistula Fundamenti* by first citing a passage subsequent to the two already treated in his former treatise.[16] After a digression from the citation of the *Thesaurus* in *nat. bon.* xliv, he once again focuses the attack on the Manichaean handbook (xlvi). To continue his critique of the *Epistula Fundamenti* with just a summary recapitulation of his previous criticism, Augustine obviously assumes his readers' familiarity with *Contra epistulam fundamenti*. Moreover, instead of giving a full account of his refutation of the rest of *Fundamenti*, as he would with a sequel, he elects to include only what he sees as germane to the theme of his treatise—the nature of the Good.

The Perceived Manichaean View of the Good

Augustine disagrees with the Manichees on the ontological nature of the Good, but he does not dispute the idea of what the Good is at the experiential level. Here, we seek to explore Augustine's understanding of the Manichaean view of the Good illustrated from explicit statements and implicit allusions in *De natura boni.*

The Good as the Beautiful.   Of all the arguments about the nature of the Good in *De natura boni*, there is only one occurrence of what we may call Augustine's explicit statement of the Manichees' understanding of the Good. To illustrate the Manichaean misjudgment, he makes comparison between the beauty of a person and that of an ape:

> Yet in all these goods, wherever they are small when compared to the greater goods, they are called by contrary names. So the human form is beautiful since the form is greater, and by comparison the beauty of an ape is called deformity. Now this deceives the imprudent [the Manichees] as if the former were a good and the latter an evil [...].[17]

Augustine implies that the Manichees judge what is good as something aesthetically pleasing to the sight: the Good is the Beautiful and evil is the lack of it. While Augustine considers that what is beautiful only differs in degree, he thinks that the Manichees treat their sensory impressions as an absolute datum—the real cause of deception. Trying to argue in Manichaean language that what is bad is nothing but corruption, Augustine ascertains that if corruption can harm the body of an ape and make it more ugly, then what is diminished is only the "good of beauty" (*pulchritudinis bonum*) (xv). Beauty here becomes the defining qualifier for the Good.[18]

Besides Augustine's clear statement above, we also discover his understanding of the Manichaean view of the Good in the form of implicit allusions. To demonstrate the absurdity of the Manichaean assertion of *Hylè* as the evil principle,[19] Augustine recalls that the original Greek meaning of *Hylè* entails the idea of capacity for form. He concludes that "if form is a good, whence those things excelling in it are called well-formed (*formosi*), just as those excelling in beauty (*species*) are termed beautiful (*speciosi*), it is beyond doubt that the capacity for form is likewise a good."[20] Here, Augustine tries to link "the good" to "the beautiful" via "the well-formed" in order to argue that *Hylè* as having capacity for form (a specific notion of beauty) is nevertheless a good in Manichaean terms.[21] Hence, Augustine implies that the Manichaean belief that good (i.e., beauty) being totally absent from *Hylè* cannot be true.

In addition, Augustine intends to communicate with the Manichees in their language and adapts the aesthetic idea of the Good for advancing his own idea. In affirming that God as the incorruptible Supreme Good is worthy of contemplation, he asserts that it is incorruptible beauty (*incorruptibilis pulchritudo*) in God to which rational spirits should cleave (vi–vii). Clearly, the beauty Augustine has in mind here is no longer that which is impressing on the physical senses, but the beauty which must be spiritually and rationally discerned. The same is said about things in the temporal order. According to Augustine, order together with measure and form is good (iii). For that reason, when one perceives order in a well-composed discourse, one will appreciate its beauty despite the transitoriness of its constituting sounds and syllables (viii).

Principle of judgment. The concept of the Good as the Beautiful automatically invites one to ask a corollary question about the principle of judgment.[22] Especially from the first of the above illustrations, it seems clear to Augustine that the Manichaean judgment of the Good depends on whether a certain thing appeals to the physical senses. Thus, pleasure to the senses becomes the governing principle of appropriation. This pleasure presupposes serenity and peace. This point may be inferred from Augustine's comment on the Manichaean attitude toward pain and suffering in the following sentence fragment: "Even pain, which some [the Manichees] regard as especially evil, whether it be in the mind or the body, [...]."[23] Presumably, the Manichees want to avoid pain of any sort at all cost because it is hurtful. This explains the parallel Augustine uses in his defence of the legitimacy of eternal fire as punishment: light is not evil because it *hurts* the weak-eyed just as eternal fire is not evil because it torments the damned, when considered from the perspective of maintaining the righteous order (xxxviii). Thus, to the Manichees, pain is deemed evil because suffering is the opposite of pleasure.[24]

Moreover, the understanding that peace is assumed in the notion of pleasure may be deduced from Augustine's polemic against the Manichaean myth[25] of the powers of darkness:

> [The Manichees] say [...] that they [the Princes of darkness] sensed each other and the light near them; that they had eyes with which they may see the light from afar [...]; that in sweetness their pleasure is enjoyed to the full; [...]. Unless there had been some sort of beauty, they would not have loved their mates [...]. Unless there was some sort of peace, they would not have obeyed their leaders.[26]

When this passage is compared with the Coptic Manichaean *Psalm to Heracleides*, we may conclude that the juxtaposition of the three notions of "light," "beauty," and "peace" is not accidental:

> Be thou like the sun, o faithful man (*pistos*), for he
>   does not

[say]: 'Fair am I', though the Lights are a thing of
                    beauty. But thou,

if thou wouldest be like thy Father, —fair are [others]
glorifying in thee and thou holding thy peace.[27]

This psalm considers the lights as something beautiful, and those who contemplate the Father of Light will have peace. In view of this understanding, we might interpret Augustine's passage as follows: When the (beautiful) light is apprehended by the powers of darkness, they feel pleasure (*uoluptas*) in their senses; when the beautiful bodies of their mates are viewed, love (with pleasure) is engendered; but in all that, some kind of peace must be present in the apprehending subject.[28]

Curiously, the Manichaean *Thesaurus* asserts, as Augustine reports it, that this aspect of peace is lacking in the powers of darkness. It is said that the beautiful bodies of the transformed powers of light inflame the lustful concupiscence of the powers of darkness (xliv). As such, although some kind of pleasure is still the mode of appropriation of what is beautiful, this pleasure is no longer peaceful but is turbulent with desires. This interpretation is in harmony with the preceding polemic of Augustine who argues that a kind of peace must be present with the powers of darkness.

Concept of evil. If Augustine understands the Manichaean idea of the Good as the Beautiful apprehended with peaceful pleasure, then what about the contrary idea of evil? As we have just demonstrated, the Manichees took pain as evil because it is hurtful and that the powers of darkness are evil by reason of their inner strife. These correspond to the physical and the spiritual aspects of evil that Augustine puts succinctly in an opening statement of the treatise:

> [The Manichees] are disturbed by the wickedness of spirit and the mortality of body, and so against this they endeavour to introduce another nature (that of malignant spirit and mortal body) which God has not made.[29]

These two aspects of evil are distinguished by Augustine as intrinsic and extrinsic. The extrinsic evil of pain may not be bad after all if it can serve the purpose of promoting a higher good, such as removing wickedness in terms of justice or repentance, whereas the intrinsic evil of wickedness must be reckoned as truly harmful.[30] In his critique of the Manichaean notion of evil, Augustine therefore remarks: "But evils [in the sense of sin] without pain are worse; for it is worse to rejoice in wickedness than to suffer from corruption."[31]

In *De Pulchro et Apto*

What we see in *De natura boni* was in fact already present in his first work, written as a Manichaean hearer. Although *De pulchro et apto* was no longer extant when he wrote *conf.* IV (around 397), Augustine leaves us with clues about his intention in writing as well as a rough idea of the content. Since all of our information about this treatise comes from his recounting, there is a concern about the strategy to isolate the raw material itself from his mature reflection of it.[32] Would Augustine have reread his Neoplatonism into his account? This question is far from settled. But even if he did, it does not necessarily follow that the data regarding his Manichaean experience is significantly tainted. Augustine's effort to show his readers exactly what he went through in the writing and thinking process during the composition of *De pulchro et apto* helps alleviate our fear. This effort reflects his intention to preserve as much as possible the true picture of his past struggle. In addition, we may be assured by the continuity of ideas between this earliest work and his dialogues.[33]

Motive of Composition

Augustine recalls that he was twenty-six or twenty-seven years old when he wrote *De pulchro et apto* (*conf.* IV.xv.27). That fixes the date of composition at about 380. He was just one or at most two years away from leaving Manichaeism (i.1). Even though at this time Augustine might have already raised serious questions about the consistency of the system,[34] he seems to believe that he still might seek the attainment of the happy life within the general Manichaean framework.[35]

Manichaean way of happy life. We will illustrate this point by appealing first to the internal evidence from the context and content of his recall of *De pulchro et apto* in *conf.* IV (the chapter where he speaks of his Manichaean sojourn), and then to the external evidence that the Manichees did have a sense of searching for happy life.

In the prelude to his mention of *De pulchro et apto*, Augustine exhorts his soul to love God, although the soul may find pleasure in bodily things (cf. Manichaeism) or in other souls (cf. friends) because otherwise one will not find rest or happy life (xii.18). Then he tells his soul that the way to *ascend* to God is through the Son who descends from heaven (xii.19). He admits his ignorance of the higher beauty of this spiritual truth at the time he wrote *De pulchro et apto*. Instead, he asked questions about the lower beauties of things (xiii.20). Put in the context of the prelude, Augustine's first account of this writing project appears to suggest that it is his attempt to seek rest or happy life by pursuing the Manichaean theme of the Beautiful.

This intention is confirmed by the inductive approach of ascent and the object of pursuit in his investigation.[36] Starting from careful observation of beautiful bodies, he proceeds to classify his results, inferring abstract qualities deemed to constitute beauty, with a view to finally being able to arrive at the Supreme Good of peaceful unity (xv.24). In retrospect, Augustine tells us of his intention in studying the nature of beauty: "desiring to stand fast and hear you, and to rejoice with joy because of the voice of the bridegroom."[37] In those days, he missed the truth which he found as a Christian but his desire to arrive at it and to rejoice in it was genuine.

The search for happy life in Manichaeism is not Augustine's own peculiar understanding. In the *Epistula Fundamenti*, the kingdom of light is said to be founded "upon bright and happy land" (*supra lucidam et beatam terram*) (*fund.* xiii; *nat. bon.* xlii). In the Psalm to Heracleides (cited above),[38] the faithful man is exhorted to be like the sun by being like the Father of Light. This person does not only have others to glory in him or her but also has peace. The attainment of peace or rest, which is the object of happy life, at least as understood by Augustine (e.g., *conf.* IV.xii.18), is obviously the expected benefit of the Manichaean worshippers.

The truth to be loved. Augustine with his searching intellect was not satisfied with what he was taught about the Manichaean fancies; he wanted to know the "truth"—the nature of beauty—even while staying within the general Manichaean framework (xv.24). Put in modern language, the writing of *De pulchro et apto* is a demythologization project, a philosophical investigation into the "truth" symbolized by the Manichaean myth.[39] Therefore, Augustine put these questions to his friends: "Do we not love anything except what is beautiful? What then is a beautiful thing? And what is beauty? What is it which entices us and wins us over to the things that we love? Unless there were grace and beauty in them, in no way could they move us."[40] He intends to find out what exactly incites the love for things considered beautiful.

It is certainly correct to identify *De pulchro et apto* as a treatise on love.[41] But this is not to overlook the fact that Augustine was indeed searching for truth as the worthy object of love. His comment on the dedication of the work to Hierius in *conf.* IV.xiv.21–23 is just a side issue, but one which touches the core of the matter: his desire to search for the ultimate truth worthy of love. But despite his effort to strain toward the Truth, he was unable to know it (xv.24, 27). Nothing could help the search, not even Aristotle's *Ten Categories*, as long as he was bound by the materialistic mode of thinking (xvi.28–31).[42]

Sketch of Content

In composing *De pulchro et apto*, Augustine took an inductive approach in a three-stage investigation: observation, abstraction, and contemplation.

Observation. The first stage consists of careful observation of physical bodies and their resulting classifications: that which is beautiful by itself (*pulchrum*) and that which is such by being suitable (*aptum*). Augustine seems to consider that this is his most important contribution in his study. This is so central that he entitles his work accordingly, and then he repeats the idea several times over (xiii.20, xiv.23, xv.24, 27). The fact that Augustine supplies examples to illustrate and support his case suggests that it is a methodical and laborious study (xv.24). It is deemed necessary because he will build his next stage of investigation upon this finding.

No doubt, Augustine's concern for the theme of beauty comes from Manichaeism,[43] but this does not deny that he uses a Platonic vehicle when he explores that theme by means of the notions of *pulchrum* and *aptum*. As with other ideas, Augustine's own contribution is evident. The two ideas of *pulchrum* and *aptum* appear in Plato's dialogues, especially *Hippias Major* 290c and 292d ff. Nevertheless, it is doubtful that Augustine got his idea directly from that piece of work instead of through other Platonic sources.[44] Even if Augustine did read Plato directly, he did not borrow straight from the book since *pulchrum* and *aptum* were coined by reducing Plato's threefold notion of beauty: a thing is deemed beautiful "because it forms a certain unity" or "because its parts are well disposed to one another" or "because the object itself, as a whole, is aptly and commodiously related to some other object." Augustine assigned the first two meanings to *pulchrum* and the last to *aptum*.[45] Moreover, Plato's Greek terms do not exactly match those of Augustine. Despite the correspondence between *to kalon* and the Latin term *pulchrum*, Plato's *to prepon* should be translated *decens* instead of *aptum*. Analyzing Augustine's later writings, Fontanier concludes instead that *pulchrum* is *decens* by itself and *aptum* is *decens* by relating to other parts.[46] Yet this point should not be pushed too far because Augustine appears to contrast *pulchrum* with *deceret* in *conf.* IV.xiii.20. On the other hand, it has been argued that here Augustine took a Ciceronian detour. He uses the example of "shoe fitting" in *De finibus* III.46, to illustrate the concept of *aptum*.[47] This and other more obvious references to *aptum* in *De finibus* and in *De oratore*, however, do not seem to bear directly on corporeal beauty, but on morality and speech.[48] Nevertheless, it is possible that Augustine gave Cicero's category a new subject content.[49] Even though it may be premature to close the question on the issue of Platonic or Ciceronian influence,[50] it is reasonable to suspect that Augustine does import the Ciceronian moral overtone into his notion of *aptum*.[51]

Abstraction. The second stage of Augustine's investigation is a reduction analysis that abstracts and isolates the qualities which he thinks the Manichees believe to be contributing to beauty—lines, colors, and expanding quantities (*conf.* IV.xv.24). Manichaeism, as understood by Augustine, does talk about colors, geometrical shapes and extension. The Manichees believe that divine particles exist in vegetables with a shiny appearance because of their bright color (*mor.* II.xvi.39). The sun with no explicit explanation is said to shine through a window of triangular shape in heaven (*Faus.* XX.6). And we are told that the region of light and the region of darkness are spatially extended, the latter having a wedge shape driven into the former. In Augustine's sarcastic illustration, it is like a piece of bread made into four equal parts, three white joined together and conceived to extend infinitely upward and sideway to form the region of light, and the one black part thought to be extended infinitely downward to form the region of darkness (*fund.* xx–xxi). By admitting that his false opinion regarding spiritual things hindered him from discerning the truth (*conf.* IV.xv.24), Augustine seems to have followed the Manichaean route of materialistic thinking, though with one important difference. He does away with the vulgar and mythological elements; lines, colors, and expanding quantities are treated as analytical categories supposed to be derived from his observations. Thus, the Platonic vehicle of ascent from material to intellectual objects is clearly at work here, involving mental activity.[52]

Contemplation. The third stage of inquiry is the arrival at the truth of the nature of beauty. Through contemplation, Augustine integrates the result of his foregoing analysis and his preference for inner peace. He concludes that the nature of the Supreme Good, the basis of beauty, lies in unity, which engenders peace of mind in him.[53] This is presumably the pure and sexless mind which Augustine called a *monad*, as against the turbulent and lustful mind *dyad*.[54] Despite the use of the Platonic vehicle of ascent, he clearly admits his position of ontological dualism (xv.24). In view of Augustine's inductive approach, it is fair to assume that his conclusion about *pulchrum* and *aptum* contributes directly to his idea that unity is the defining character for the nature of the Supreme Good. Whether it is beauty as a whole or beauty by reason of suitability, the concept of unity underlies both. Moreover, Augustine would have identified the Supreme Good to be the good principle in Manichaeism,[55] but in consideration of his demythologization program it is doubtful that he would believe it to be the Father of Light. Augustine's juxtaposition of terms shows that his conception of Supreme Good at this time remains an intellectual category. Therefore, in closing he recalls that he had not yet known that his mind is not the "supreme and unchangeable good" (*summum atque incommutabile bonum*) (xv.24). To identify the locale of unity, he again places three terms in appositional relation: rational mind (*mens rationalis*), nature of truth (*natura ueritatis*), and nature of the Supreme Good (*natura summi boni*) (xv.24). This suggests that the Supreme Good or the truth resides with the rational mind.

Augustine's Early Idea of the Good

To look for Augustine's idea of the Good at this point, we must again come to the notion of Supreme Good which is the truth. But as just shown, this truth is no less than the truth concerning the nature of beauty, the object of pursuit in order to attain happiness. Therefore, it is clear in Augustine's mind that the Good is the Beautiful. On the other hand, in regard to the principle of judgment, Augustine in his address to his friends equates beauty with that which "entices us and wins us over" (*nos allicit et conciliat*) (xiii.20). Here, pleasure to the senses is not mentioned but assumed. In the context of ascent, the contemplating subject's aim is to arrive at the peace of mind engendered in unity. Once again the idea of serene pleasure is what Augustine was after in his search for the truth of the nature of beauty. This directly contrasts what he considered as the evil mind or *dyad* that is involved in "anger in cruel acts and lust in shameful deeds" (*ira in facinoribus, libido in flagitiis*) (xv.24). While the two dispositions are different in expression they are actually similar in kind, for both are turbulent or, in Augustine's own vocabulary, *discordia* (xv.24). Therefore, compared with the Manichaean idea of the Good portrayed in the later *De natura boni,* Augustine's early conception shows no significant difference. In the context of the search for an understanding of happy life, how does this concept of the Good influence Augustine's view of the Supreme Good? That is our next question.

CHAPTER THREE

NOTION OF SUPREME GOOD

Augustine's Idea of Supreme Good

Augustine's treatment of the idea of Supreme Good is a continuation of his former search for happy life while still a Manichaean hearer. To prove this point, we first identify what constitutes his idea of Supreme Good in both his earliest and latest anti-Manichaean treatises and then trace the inception of the development of this idea to its Manichaean influence in *De beata uita.*

In *De Natura Boni*

The term "Supreme Good" (*summum bonum*) is used in many places but Augustine succinctly summarizes its meaning in the opening sentences of *De natura boni* (i) as "The Supreme Good, above which there is nothing, is God. And for this reason, it is immutable good, truly eternal, truly immortal."[1] In a word, "Supreme Good" to him is that good which exists immutably. However, Augustine's idea of good is further qualified by "measure, form, order" (*modus, species, ordo*) (iii).[2] Hence, "Supreme Good" is that which cannot be corrupted, in the sense that its original measure, form and order always remain the same (vi). As anything other than God exists because its own measure (*modus*) remains in it, God as the Supreme Good may be called supreme measure (*summus modus*) in terms of his self-defining measure that is independent of any external factor:

> We may neither say that God has measure, in case that is taken to mean his limit, nor may we say therefore that he is without measure by whom measure is given to all things in order that by some measure they may exist, nor should we again say that God has measure, as if he should receive measure from something. Yet, if we call him the supreme measure, we say something important, if we understand by what we call

supreme measure the Supreme Good, for all measure, in so far as it is measure, is good. From that, we cannot speak of things as moderate, modest or modified without implying praise [...].[3]

From this quotation, we may conclude that Augustine's idea of the Supreme Good is inherently linked to measure, so much so that he calls the former supreme measure. As the Supreme Good confers existence on corporeal things by giving them measure (xxi), it also preserves rational beings from corruption and grants them happiness by their contemplation of the incorruptible beauty (*incorruptibilis pulchritudo*) of the Supreme Good (vii–viii). Here, Augustine's notion of Supreme Good consists of two aspects: its supreme existence which is different from the existence of other things; and its granting of happiness to rational beings. As we will see, these aspects have already been developed in Augustine's earliest anti-Manichaean writings in relation to the concept of God as supreme measure.

In Earlier Anti-Manichaean Writings

As indicated in *De natura boni*, the assertion of the immutability of the Supreme Good is Augustine's obvious attempt to counter the Manichaean view of the nature of good and evil (*nat. bon.* i–ii). This polemic is first developed in *De moribus Manichaeorum*, but seminal ideas may be traced back to still earlier works in *De Genesi contra Manichaeos* and *De moribus ecclesiae Catholicae*. In *De moribus Manichaeorum*, Augustine reasons that the supreme and original existence (*summe ac primitus esse*) of the Supreme Good guarantees its immutability (*mor.* II.i.1). In comparison, all created things are mutable and are good in as much as they participate in the Supreme Good (iv.6). The harmony of the former is an imitation of the unity of the latter (vi.8). Only a little earlier, in *De Genesi contra manichaeos*,[4] Augustine explains that this harmony is governed by measure, number, and order (*mensura et numerus et ordo*) which are derived from supreme measure, number, and order (*a summa mensura et numero et ordine*) that lie in the immutable and eternal sublimity of God (I.xvi.26). It has been suggested that the three terms in apposition reflect the trinitarian structure of created being. Augustine here quotes Wis. 11:21 for the first time to show that God disposed all things in measure, number, and weight. In order to fit the wording of the quoted verse, Augustine may have replaced *mensura* for *modus*.[5] Hence, *summus modus* may be considered a synonym of *summa mensura* which is distinguished from created things by its supreme existence. But besides being an anti-Manichaean polemic, this requirement of supreme existence for the Supreme Good has its root context in the pursuit of happy life of the early Augustine. The link is the two qualifications for the Supreme Good: it must be that beyond which there is no higher good, and it must be that which cannot be adversely affected (*mor.* II.iii.5).

We find the same two points emphasized earlier in *mor.* I.iii.5,[6] and these conditions can only be satisfied by God who must be loved as the measure of love in himself (*ipse dilectionis modus*). This love which is appropriate for God is our supreme love for God (*summus amor dei*) because he is the Supreme Good (viii.13). Here, in the context of love for God, the measure for the Supreme Good is supreme measure. But what is love for God except the enjoyment of him who makes one happy (iii.4, 5)?[7] This happiness is attained when one has inner peace through the Son, the wisdom of God (xvi.27). For that reason, God the Father who is the Supreme Good is also called supreme wisdom and supreme peace (xxiv.44). While God as supreme peace is a reminder of the benefits he confers on the contemplator, God as supreme wisdom is a projected designation from the Son being the wisdom of God. From Augustine's consideration that wisdom is the measure of the soul,[8] supreme wisdom would be equivalent to supreme measure.

As in *De natura boni*, the above notion of supreme measure is the result of Augustine's investigation in *De beata uita*. In what is to follow, we will first look for indications of continuity of the framework within which the earliest idea of Supreme Good is developed, in view of locating the role of *De beata uita*. Then, we will argue the following point: In light of the consideration that the Supreme Good is the guarantor of happy life, the requirements of its immutable existence and of its ability to promote tranquility are due to the contributing influence of Augustine's understanding of the Manichaean concept of the Good.

"Supreme Good" in the Frame of "Happy Life"

It is reasonable to ask why Augustine uses the search for happy life as the first polemical vehicle in his anti-Manichaean writings. As we are told, he tries to speak at the level of his audience with rational arguments, instead of invoking authority, to convince those who are influenced by Manichaeism that the Christian God alone is the means to the attainment of happy life (*mor.* I.ii.3–iii.4). Augustine assumes that the issue of happy life is one that interests his audience (iii.4), not only as human persons, but perhaps especially as persons who might be enticed by the Manichaean teaching of the blissful kingdom of light.[9] Having gone through the struggle of a search for happy life which led him from Manichaeism to Christianity, he might have believed that the route of inquiry that has brought him to the resting place of the Christian faith would also help convince those in a similar situation—those who are open to and desire the truth—either to stay away from Manichaeism or to leave it for Christianity.[10]

The content of *De moribus ecclesiae Catholicae* thus should reflect the result of Augustine's earlier attempt to search for happy life, no longer as a Manichaean hearer but as a new convert to the Christian faith. That his quest did not stop at the time of his conversion is related by Augustine in the first chapter of *De beata uita*. Before the conversion, he was like the last of the three classes of seafarers who desire to arrive at the port of rest, the region of happy life. Then, he was not free of the mists and for quite a while was led astray with his eyes fixed on "those stars that sink into the ocean" (*labentia in Oceanum astra*) (i.4). The childish superstition he was subscribing to at that point is obviously Manichaeism for it relates to a time prior to his crossing over to the Academics (i.4).[11] By the time Augustine wrote *De beata uita*, although he had arrived at the land of rest and had learned to know "the North Star" (i.4), he was still searching for the exact part of the land where he could find real happiness (i.5). It was this search that occasioned the subsequent disputation, Augustine's attempt at a "focused" search for happy life in the context of his newly acquired Christian faith.[12]

Manichaean Traces

After his conversion to Christianity, Augustine does not only intend to adhere to a consistent framework in the early development of "Supreme Good," his approach to the idea via the concept of measure, despite the use of Neoplatonic vehicles, is due in part to his notion of the Good gained as a Manichaean hearer. We will explore Augustine's development of the idea of Supreme Good in *De beata uita* with reference to relevant concepts appearing in *Contra Academicos*.[13] The objective is to show that supreme measure is the answer to his original quest of the Supreme Good in *De pulchro et apto*.

The Content of True Beauty

As previously shown, Augustine's understanding of the Manichaean idea of the Good is the Beautiful. It is beauty defined as that which pleases the physical senses and engenders peace of mind. In the context of the pursuit of happy life in *De pulchro et apto*, we saw that the "Manichaean" Augustine understood the Supreme Good as the final goal of contemplation that is supposed to give the mind tranquil pleasure.

Augustine, after his conversion to Christianity, never denied beauty as the route to attainment of happy life, except that he clarifies what the true content of beauty is supposed to be. As mapped out in *Contra Academicos*, this involves linking sensible beauty to philosophy in its etymological sense (*acad.* II.iii.7). There, Augustine distinguishes three notions of beauty: sensible beauty, reflected beauty or philocaly, and philosophy.

Sensible and reflected beauty. Already in *De pulchro et apto*, Augustine ascribes an object's beauty to its unity in wholeness (*pulchrum*) or in suitability (*aptum*) to its environment. As Augustine indicates later in *mor.* II.vi.8, these two concepts are inherently related: *aptum* is an imitation of *pulchrum*. There in his earliest writing, the "Platonic concept"[14] of order as a constitutive factor of beauty is assumed in Augustine's assertion of the Manichaean theme of the Good as the Beautiful. The same argument is followed up in his first post-conversion treatise. In *acad.* II.ii.6, Augustine points out that there is another kind of beauty behind the outwardly beautiful appearance of seashore resorts, parks, banquets, and theatrical exhibitions that incite sensible pleasure. This other beauty indeed sometimes emerges as true beauty (*uera pulchritudo*). Though often hidden amidst vices and errors, it is plainly visible to a few who look intently and diligently enough beyond the mere "presentability" (*mundissima facies*) of things. Whether this true beauty can be seen as it really is depends on the disposition—the mental adornment in addition to perseverance—of the perceiving subject, because it is a reflected beauty, which Augustine calls "the appearance of philosophy" (*facies philosophiae*).

Philocaly and philosophy. The branch of study of beauty commonly known as philocaly is akin to philosophy for, according to Augustine, they have a common lineage, although, of the two, only philosophy is the pure form of true beauty without any entanglement in appearances. Augustine comments:

> [...] philocaly and philosophy have very similar surnames, as if they are of (and they want to be seen as) the same family. In fact, what is philosophy? It is love of wisdom. And what is philocaly? It is love of beauty. Consult the Greeks about this. But what, then, is wisdom? Is it not the true beauty itself? Therefore, those two are absolutely true siblings, begotten of the same parent. But the former was enticed from her lofty position in the sky by the allurement of lust, and was shut up in a common cage. Nevertheless, she retained the similarity of name, in

order to remind her captor not to despise her. Thus, the sister that flies
freely often recognizes this wingless one who is mourning and in need
(yet she seldom sets her free), for no one except philosophy knows from
where philocaly derives her lineage.[15]

Since Augustine identifies *philos* (love) as the common lineage, he
perceives both philosophy and philocaly as rooted in the subject's
determination with regard to the object to be contemplated. In his
understanding of Manichaeism, the Beautiful is determined by the
subject's judgment of what gives the mind tranquil pleasure. In view of
Augustine's Manichaean past, it is reasonable to suspect that when he
considered the entrapment of philocaly, he was hinting at the Manichees'
failed attempt to transcend the sensible beauty that results in the creation
of phantasms.[16] Now, philosophy as love of wisdom, being free from the
stumbling block of philocaly, has become the answer to Augustine's long
search for true beauty that goes back to his Manichaean years.[17]

Wisdom as the Measure of the Soul

How has philosophy become Augustine's answer, or to put it plainly,
What does wisdom have to do with the soul's enjoyment of tranquil
pleasure? Augustine considers wisdom as the soul's measure (*modus*),[18] in
the sense that with it the soul attains its full existence in equilibrium (*sese
animus librat*).[19] It is neither in excess as the soul is inflated with luxuries,
despotism and pride nor in lack as the miserable soul experiences
meanness, fear, grief, or passion (*beat. uit.* iv.33). Augustine considers that
the soul's tranquility consists in its being healthy,[20] that is, the soul attains
to the fullness of its set limit.

He strengthens this idea by introducing the term *frugalitas* or
"frugality" to explain *modus* (ii.8; iv.31–32). In view of the assumption of
the Manichaean idea of the Good in Augustine's effort to make a
connection between sensible beauty and philosophy (love of wisdom), it is
reasonable to believe that the same assumption is at work behind his veiled
attempt to link beauty to *frugalitas* when he attributes restraint and
frugalitas to the great and most beautiful part of virtue (*Cuius [uirtus]
magna pars est atque pulcherrima, quae temperantia et frugalitas dicitur*)
(ii.8). What amounts to beauty then is due not only to the orderly
arrangement of things but also to the virtuous condition of the soul that
maintains an orderly equilibrium. Such is the condition from which the
soul derives enjoyment because *frugalitas*, as deliberately underscored by
Augustine, is inherently tied to its root idea of *fructus* (enjoyment) (ii.8).
Also, from the productive notion of *fructus,* spiritual fecundity is implied
in *frugalitas.*[21] It seems clear that one reason Augustine connects the

Ciceronian concept of *frugalitas* to the Plotinian notion of restraint (*temperantia*) (*Enn.* I.ii.6) is that he wants to develop the idea of enjoyment as pleasure in moderation (*modus*),[22] the result of the soul's possession of wisdom as true beauty. This emphasis on moderation is well demonstrated in Augustine's qualification of the subjective disposition of one who attains the happy life. The condition is moderation of desires (*cupiendi modus*), or in other words enjoyment (*perfruatur*) with proper and pleasant contentment (ii.11). In this way, the contributing influence of the Manichaean motif of beauty (that which engenders tranquil pleasure), expressed in Ciceronian and Plotinian terms, on Augustine's conception of wisdom as the soul's *modus*, remains clearly visible.

Guarantor of Tranquil Pleasure

In Augustine's pursuit of happy life in *De pulchro et apto*, "Supreme Good" is understood as the truth concerning the nature of beauty that guarantees tranquil pleasure of the soul. This notion of Supreme Good as the guarantor of tranquil enjoyment carries over to *De beata uita* where the notion is implicitly assumed in the initial discussion of happy life and is explicitly identified as supreme measure at the end of the investigation. There, the guarantor role of the Supreme Good is both negatively considered as a necessary condition and positively developed as a sufficient condition for the attainment of happy life.[23]

Prevention of loss of tranquil pleasure. Negatively considered, according to Augustine, the Supreme Good as an object of desire which can be enjoyed must be a subsistent object that cannot be lost against one's will, for when one suffers loss or even only fears loss of the object of desire one cannot be happy (*beat. uit.* ii.11, iv.26–27). Therefore, the logical conclusion is that the Supreme Good as the desired object must have fullness of existence so that it always remains (*semper manens*) (ii.11). Augustine associates the idea of existence (*esse*) with that which remains (*manet*), stands firm (*constat*), always the same (*semper tale est*) and carefully defines it again in terms of *frugalitas* in contrast to *nequitia* (wickedness) (ii.8, vi.30–31), to mean substantial subsistence: "substantial" because of fullness and "capable of subsisting" when there is an ordering measure (*modus*) to keep things from degenerating. In his qualification of *modus* as fullness of existence,[24] Augustine accords much emphasis to the two related ideas of *temperantia* (i.e., restraint) and *frugalitas*, which are distinguished from the uncontrolled *abundantia* (ii.8; iv.31–32).[25] Although the notion of fullness is relevant, that of limit is not, when applied to God. Thus, in his designation of God as supreme measure,

Augustine circumvents the problem by asserting that God in self-reference is his own measure: *summus modus per summum modum modus est* (iv.34).[26] As such, the idea of fulfillment of measure as fullness of existence is assured without the imposition of an external limit. For the contemplator, this stability of existence of the Supreme Good as supreme measure is necessary to guarantee the soul's tranquil enjoyment of it.

Assurance of tranquil pleasure.   Positively considered, the Supreme Good as having its fullness of existence is the ground for all orderly existence, not only of irrational objects but also of rational beings. By the steady inner presence of God, the Supreme Good, one can be made happy (iii.17) by one's enablement to enjoy God (*deo perfrui*) (iv.34). The reason is that this Supreme Good is supreme measure, and as such God confers measure to individuals through the Son.

Here, Augustine broaches a theory of the Trinity. He identifies the Son of God as the wisdom (measure of the soul) who mediates between the Father (the supreme measure) and humankind in terms of measure. Doignon suggests that the transition from "wisdom" to "the Son of God" is an example of Augustine's dual approach of "reason" and "authority" employed in his early dialogues (see also *De ordine* II.v.16). The transition takes place in three stages. By means of philosophical argument and classical inspiration from Cicero, Augustine arrives at the point that possession of wisdom is the key to a happy life. Then, he points out that wisdom should be properly called wisdom of God. And finally, by appealing to divine authority, Augustine takes one step further to identify this wisdom of God with the second person of the Trinity. Reasoning that *Quae* instead of *Quid* is used as an interrogative pronoun to refer to "wisdom" in *beat. uit.* iv.34, Doignon even argues that before referring to "wisdom of God" (*Dei sapientia*), Augustine has already treated "wisdom" as personal.[27]

The Son, who is also the Truth, emanates from supreme measure and converts back to it.[28] And the person who attains to supreme measure through the Son has happy life (iv.34). The Holy Spirit is not explicitly mentioned in this work, but a trinitarian structure is vaguely discernible in the final admonition: To have happy life is "to know piously and perfectly, by whom you are led into the truth, that truth you enjoy to the full, and through which you are connected to supreme measure."[29] Since the fulfillment of the soul's measure is essential to its attainment of tranquil pleasure. In contemplating God the supreme measure, we are assured of tranquil enjoyment of him through the active trinitarian operation.

In regard to the idea of Supreme Good, what we call the negative consideration is a concern for its immutability and the positive consideration is an issue of its conference of beatitude, both thematized by the notion of supreme measure that appears in *De natura boni* and in the two books of *De moribus*. In both considerations, God as supreme measure is shown to be the guarantee of the soul's tranquil enjoyment of him, a role reminiscent of that of the Supreme Good in Augustine's *De pulchro et apto*. Or indeed, in the notion of supreme measure, he has found his answer to the initial quest of the Supreme Good.

Plotinian Vehicle for a Manichaean Notion

There remains one last question: Could the idea of tranquil enjoyment of the Supreme Good come directly from Plotinus' concept of contemplation of the supreme beauty instead of Augustine's understanding of the Manichaean notion of the Good as the Beautiful? To answer this question, we need to investigate how Augustine has modified the Plotinian vehicle of contemplation in view of his Manichaean notion. We only need to summarize some of the points touched on in the preceding discussion into a coherent statement.

Evidence. It is true that other than the Manichees, Plotinus also attributes beauty to the Supreme Good and calls it supreme beauty in the context of ecstatic contemplative experience (*Enn.* I.vi.7). The important question is, however, to ask why Augustine in his search for the Supreme Good emphasizes so much the Ciceronian idea of measure (*modus*),[30] and hence God as supreme measure, a concept only implicitly traceable to Plotinus' dominant notion of *the One*.[31] In contrast to ecstasy in the encounter of the Plotinian supreme beauty, the contemplative experience of supreme measure is moderate enjoyment. Hence, instead of asking us to plunge into union with God in ecstatic love,[32] Augustine's admonition to enjoy (*perfrui*) God (*beat. uit.* iv.34) means to remember, to seek, and to thirst after Him tirelessly (iv.35). Even when Augustine speaks of our supreme love for God, it is to be understood in terms of this manner of enjoyment of God.[33] Augustine's consideration of moderation (*modus*) may be shown to be due to the import of his Manichaean idea of tranquil pleasure, the principle of judgment for the Beautiful.

Root. Even four or five years before Augustine read Plotinus' *Peri tou kalou*,[34] the "Manichaean" Augustine in *De pulchro et apto* showed his concern for contemplative moderation in the context of virtue. There, the Ciceronian twist of the Platonic notion of suitability (*aptum*) might suggest that his emphasis is a moral rather than a purely aesthetic issue.[35] Thus, in Augustine's pursuit of contemplation of beauty, the virtue of the soul would be his main concern. He recalls that in searching for the Supreme Good, the peace derived from virtue becomes his signpost (*conf.* XIII.xv.24). This central regard for peace or tranquility as the manifestation of the soul's virtue in the attainment of happiness doubtless comes from the Manichaean notion of the Good as the Beautiful, or that which engenders tranquil pleasure. Such a concern for tranquility helps condition Augustine's subsequent view of contemplative experience.

Means. In this regard, the Christian Augustine attempts to link two aspects of Plotinian contemplation. Under the theme of measure, he moderates the ecstatic experience with the after-effect of contemplation—especially the realization of the virtue of restraint in the soul.[36] Thus, in *mor.* I.xix.35 Augustine believes that the virtue of restraint (*temperantia*) is the condition for the contemplative enjoyment of God's goodness, an idea traceable to *beat. uit.* ii.8–10. In order to bridge these two Plotinian aspects, Augustine introduces the Ciceronian notion of *frugalitas* which has both the idea of restraint as well as the inherent etymological implication of enjoyment.[37] In this way, the notion of enjoyment becomes synonymous with his understanding of the Manichaean idea of tranquil pleasure. It is pleasure because it is enjoyable; it is tranquil for there is restraint.

Supreme Good as the Ground of Creation

In his idea of supreme measure, Augustine is unlike Plotinus who stresses the concept of God as supreme beauty; nevertheless, Augustine's affirmation of God's fullness of existence expressed in the notion of *frugalitas* lays the groundwork for development along this line. Indeed, evidence for a direct connection between Supreme Good (as supreme measure) and beauty is not totally lacking. This is expected in view of the carry-over of Manichaean influence from *De pulchro et apto* because the undemythologized Manichaean Supreme Good would be the Father of Light who is deemed supremely beautiful.

Beauty in God's Supreme Existence

Under certain circumstances, Augustine does intend to mean that God is beautiful. In his summary statement on the nature of the Good, he mentions that in God is incorruptible beauty for our contemplation (*nat. bon.* vii), a clear evidence that supreme measure as supreme existence is tied to the idea of beauty.[38] But this is not limited to the context of contemplation. Another affirmation of beauty in supreme existence is found in Augustine's idea of supreme form (*summa forma*) (*uer. rel.* xi.21), derived from the notion of supreme measure, applied both to the re-formation of the soul and to the preservation of the cosmic beauty in creation and judgment (xi.21–xii.24, xxiii.44). Augustine's very choice of the term *forma* is intent upon associating the concept of measure with that of beauty.[39] In all these, beauty is synonymous with the fullness of existence in its proper form or measure. Connecting *forma* with the cosmic order, Augustine implies that God is beautiful not only because in his own measure he guarantees tranquil pleasure for the contemplating soul, but also in it he is the ground of all beauty in the created universe. Therefore, God as the Supreme Good is supreme existence (*summe esse*) in the sense that he not only exists immutably but also creates and orders things with *forma* and *species* (i.e., beauty) (e.g., *uer. rel.* xviii.35; *mor.* II.i.1, vi.8). As such, the whole of creation is good and beautiful.[40]

Implied Creational Aspect in "Supreme Measure"

The ideas of order and measure are not exactly the same but are closely related. "Order" is an all-embracing notion implying rationality and harmony, whereas "measure" is concerned with regulation of an individual entity. Yet both share the common connotation of existence in proper proportion, whether interior to the thing itself as in "measure" (*beat. uit.* iv.32) or exterior in relation to other entities as in "order" (*ord.* II.xiv.40, xix.49; cf. II.v.14). By linking "existence in proper proportion" with "beauty" by means of the common concept of "unity" (I.ii.3, *conf.* IV.xv.24), we conclude that Augustine's two early notions of "beauty" (*pulchrum*) and "suitability" (*aptum*) find their application here. In spite of their commonality, "measure" and "order" emerge from different contexts in the anti-Manichaean debate.

As shown earlier, "measure" originates from the discussion of the pursuit of happy life in terms of attaining tranquil pleasure. "Order," on the other hand, comes as Augustine's response to the Manichaean question about the goodness of creation. If, according to the Manichaean notion, the Good is the Beautiful, then the whole universe perceived in the unity of order must be good, and hence beautiful, despite the presence of individual evil things. The problem with the Manichees' inability to see the Good in everything created is again due to their erroneous perception, or a lack of unity of vision (*ord.* I.i.2–ii.3; *Gen. Man.* I.xvi.26). For a full discussion on this issue of the Manichaean connection, we must await the treatment of Augustine's doctrine of predestination.[41]

Although "measure" (*modus*) and "order" (*ordo*) do not have the same origin, they are put together in Augustine's development of the concept of Supreme Good as the first and the third term of a three part expression. The earliest occurrence is in the form of *mensura et numerus et ordo* (*Gen. Man.* I.xvi.26), where *mensura* is synonymous with *modus*. A later version is found to be *modus, species, ordo* (*nat. bon.* iii). In both circumstances, God is referred to as the basis. But while he is said to possess *summa mensura et numero et ordine* in the first case (*Gen. Man.* I.xvi.26), God is only called *summus modus* in the second (*nat. bon.* xxi–xxii).[42] Thus, it seems that the later reference of *summus modus* in a single term has acquired different shades of meaning—particularly that of *ordo*—when applied to God as the basis of creation. This observation reminds us that the enriched meaning of *summus modus* in *De natura boni* is not yet fully in place in the earlier *De beata uita* where the meaning was based on the idea of *frugalitas*.

The Manichaean idea of the Good as the Beautiful inspired Augustine's notion of Supreme Good. Does it also have a similar effect on his understanding of personal evil? That is our next subject of concern.

CHAPTER FOUR

CONCEPT OF PERSONAL EVIL

Two Ideas

The Manichaean explanation of the human predicament of personal sin, as understood by Augustine, is due to the admixture of good and evil in each individual. According to the Manichaean myth, the first humans are produced from certain princes of Smoke in order to trap the light particles already held by other powers of darkness (*nat. bon.* xlvi; *haer.* xlvi). In Adam's soul, therefore, it is mostly light and very little darkness (*mor.* II.xix.73) and the human body as the work of the race of darkness is intended to confine the captive deity (*Faus.* XX.22). Thus, within a human person, there are always two conflicting metaphysical principles at work that prevent one from doing good, and, as Augustine asserts, there are "two souls in one body" (*duae animae in uno corpore*) (*uer. rel.* ix.16).[1] After his conversion, although Augustine no longer subscribes to Manichaean dualism, he cannot deny the reality of the inner human struggle which occurs when one strives to do good. He resorts to explaining it in terms of the defective turning of the human will. Yet, why is there continuous defection of the will unless there is a kind of principle—or the flesh—residing in all of Adam's descendants? This similarity of view regarding the inevitability of personal evil shared by both the Manichees and Augustine has led scholars to suspect a link between the two.[2] Manichaean influence on Augustine is very possible because Augustine's attention to determinism goes against the tide of his contemporary theological climate which emphasizes free will and human responsibility.[3] Nonetheless, the search for a common historical origin between the view of the Manichees and that of Augustine has not yet been conclusive.[4] Here, we will take an alternate route to show the connection between the two views by matching Augustine's use of terminology in the context that reflects his perception of the Manichaean usage with his general employment of the same terms or their modified forms. To achieve this objective, we consider the themes of *consuetudo*[5] and *concupiscentia*.

The Concept of *Consuetudo*

In his earliest anti-Manichaean writings, Augustine employs the term *consuetudo* to accuse the Manichees of being fond of bodily pleasure and unable to break away from their carnal outlook. From the standpoint of a more direct possible Manichaean influence, however, it is in *De uera religione* (xi.21–xxiii.44) that he adapts the dual Manichaean notion of spiritual and physical evil—"wickedness" and "mortality"—in order to attempt a full theory of personal evil.[6] In this attempt, Augustine does not explicitly connect the dual notion of evil with *consuetudo*, although he mentions the term five times in the work.[7] Our task, therefore, is to show that not only is Augustine's development of the theory of personal evil built on the Manichaean insight into the Good, but also that this is a theory which explains personal evil in terms of the mechanism of *consuetudo*. To trace his adaptation of Manichaean ideas in the theory, we focus on *De uera religione*. But to establish the link between this theory and *consuetudo*, we will, in view of the conceptual development of the latter, show that 1) the theory fulfils the expectation from the discussion of *consuetudo* in anti-Manichaean writings prior to *De uera religione*, 2) the implications of the five occasional references in this work are sufficiently linked to the content of the theory, and 3) the discussion of *consuetudo* in the anti-Manichaean works immediately after *De uera religione* reflects the application of the theory.

Anticipation in Earlier Writings

The term *consuetudo* appears in *De moribus ecclesiae Catholicae* in Augustine's discussion of the virtue of fortitude—the bearing of the loss of earthly things in view of distancing oneself from bodily pleasure (xxii.40). This consideration is anti-Manichaean in nature for in their pursuit of the Good as the Beautiful that engenders bodily pleasure, the Manichees want to be shielded from physical pain at all cost (v.7). In speaking of *consuetudo*, Augustine has already shown sign of attempt at a theory to explain the incomprehensible mystery of the soul's bondage to the corruption of the body. In his own words:

> The love [...] which ought with all sanctity to be inflamed for God, is called temperate, in not seeking those [earthly] things, and strong, in losing them. But among all things which are possessed in this life, the human body, by God's most righteous laws, is the heaviest bond, due to

the sin of old, concerning which nothing is better known among things to be proclaimed, yet nothing is more mysterious among things to be comprehended. This bond, lest it be shaken or attacked, agitates the soul with the fear of labour and pain; and, in order that it not be taken away and destroyed, bothers the soul with the fear of death. For the soul loves it out of force of habit, not knowing that if used well and wisely its resurrection and reformation will, by divine activity and law, be with no difficulty made subject to its authority [...].[8]

Here, we perceive a suggestion of the inevitability of personal evil in Augustine's mention of the predicament concerning the human body, after the primal sin, as "the heaviest chain" (*grauissimum uinculum*). The problem of the soul is its inability to break loose from the inertial force of *consuetudo* for fear of suffering bodily harm. This inertia puts a biased condition on the direction of the soul's voluntary turning toward the intended object of love, in preferring one over the other. And behind this bondage is the soul's desire for bodily pleasure, as is assumed in Augustine's ideas of fortitude and temperance. Here also, the ignorance of not knowing a better alternative (i.e., to use the body well by scorning bodily pleasure) contributes to the confinement of the soul in this bondage.

Only a little later, Augustine again expounds on the concept of *consuetudo* in *De Genesi contra Manichaeos* II in his allegorical interpretation of the punishment received by the woman—which signifies the body—after the first sinning. This bodily corruption is explicitly identified as "mortality" (*mortalitas*) shared by animals and humans alike after the fall; yet, for humans, there is an added mysterious dimension of moral difficulty as punishment (xix.29). What is mysterious is the lack of explanation for the human inner struggle when a good deed is attempted. According to Augustine's observation,

> there is no withholding from carnal inclination which does not have pain in the beginning, until habit is bent toward the better part. When this has come about, it is as if a child is born, that is, through the good habit the disposition is prepared for a good work. In order that this habit be born, it struggles in pain with bad habit.[9]

The previous idea of the inertial force of evil *consuetudo* is explained as an ingrained disposition that resists any change of course for the better, at least not without struggle and pain. And what maintains this inertia is carnal inclination (*uoluntas carnalis*). The problem is the will compromised by the flesh, for the will can no longer shift direction with ease.

Besides moral difficulty, bodily corruption also results in ignorance of truth. This point is similarly expounded in Augustine's allegorical interpretation for the punishment of man—which signifies the rational soul—after the fall. Ignorance is not so much the difficulty of living rightly as it is the difficulty of discovering the truth and of resisting the error of phantasms arising through the physical senses (xx.30). With the idea of "ignorance" brought into the picture as the counterpart of "moral difficulty," we are only one step away from linking the former, as has been done with the latter, to *consuetudo*. Thus, in the immediate development in *De moribus Manichaeorum*, *consuetudo* has acquired the added aspect of ignorance in the sense of a forceful resistance to truth (ix.18, xiii.30).

We may now summarize what Augustine expects in his theory of *consuetudo*. 1) It must explain the mystery of the inevitability of evil: the soul's continuous bondage. 2) The explanation must be in the context of bodily corruption caused by the primal sin. 3) It must be formulated in terms of the function of bodily pleasure. 4) It must address the issues of both spiritual ignorance and moral difficulty (*ignorantia et difficultas*).[10] These points are expanded in *De uera religione*.

Development in *De Uera Religione*
Occasional references. There are altogether five references to *consuetudo* in *De uera religione*; each signifies the existing condition of human bondage to the power of the flesh. In mentioning "popular habit" (*consuetudo [populorum]*), Augustine conjectures the explanation Plato and other philosophers would give, if they were to come back to life again, for not teaching the people the truth found in the Christian faith. The projected answer is one of apology: they would rather yield to the *consuetudo* of the people than bring them over to faith (*fides*) and to inclination (*uoluntas*) for heavenly things (*uer. rel.* iv.6). By putting faith and its related inclination in opposition to popular *consuetudo*, Augustine would imply that *consuetudo* is the way of life that cannot rise above spiritual darkness and subjugation to the love of earthly things. The assumption of both *ignorantia* and *difficultas* is vaguely visible. This condition is well captured by James Wetzel's comment about the meaning of *consuetudo*, which cannot be fully translated by either "custom" or "habit." For him, the term actually refers to

> the formation of a person's character out of the patterns of interplay between wanton desires and half-wanton sensibilities. The wanton part makes it a little less than custom, and the half-wanton part makes it a little more than habit. As long as a person remains *ante legem*,

consuetudo continues to constrict the possibilities for character change.[11]

A person in this condition is not necessarily unruly but is unable to reflect on and critique the (spiritual) situation he or she is in.

Of the two aspects of *ignorantia* and *difficultas*, however, *consuetudo* sometimes seems to be primarily referring to the first term,[12] as is implied in the following lines:

> So long as it [the soul] is wounded by love of things that come and go, and by pain [at losing them], so long as it is devoted to the habit of this life (*consuetudo huius uitae*) and to the bodily senses, and fades among empty images [...].[13]

From the above parallel structure, *consuetudo* is aligned with bodily senses (*sensus corporis*) in contrast to the love and loss of material things. Nonetheless, *consuetudo* can never be separated from the notion of worldly desires. Indeed, there is a connection between *consuetudo* and pride, or self-love, which may be understood as the root of the desire for satisfying bodily pleasure in fallen humans.[14] Augustine tells us that it is hard to be able to find an earthling who can resist "human habit" (*consuetudo hominum*) and human praise (*laus hominum*) (xxxiv.64). Moreover, since the struggle occurs in the mind, Augustine warns Romanianus, the recipient of *De uera religione*, not to "strive" (*certare*) to behold truth by self-effort in case he should be deceived by phantasms. Presumably, only by God's grace may one "conquer" (*uincere*) that "bodily habit" (*consuetudo corporum*) and be victorious (xxxv.65). The use of military language underlines the force of *consuetudo* in operation. Augustine furthermore admonishes us to love—but not carnally, for all such relations are contingent upon time. Rather, to be fit for the kingdom of God, one must resist "carnal habit" (*consuetudo carnalis*) (xlvi.88). Here, *consuetudo* is explicitly linked to the flesh.

Comparing with references to *consuetudo* in the earlier works, we perceive here a possible development of the ideas of "ignorance" and "moral difficulty." Through this development, Augustine might have attempted at explaining the phenomenon of struggle in the soul, and at raising the issues about self-love and the central role of the flesh. A substantial treatment on the notion of personal evil could be emerging in *De uera religione*.

The Manichaean connection. Although Augustine disagrees with the Manichees concerning the nature of evil as substantial, he is more in tune with them in terms of understanding the subjective experience of it.

Earlier, we observed that in *De natura boni*, Augustine understands the Manichaean notion of evil, in contrast to the idea of the Good as the Beautiful that engenders peaceful pleasure, as loss of tranquility, and it is categorized respectively in spiritual and physical senses as "wickedness" and "mortality." These are recognized by Augustine as intrinsic and extrinsic evils. While the former is truly harmful, the latter is blessing in disguise, if it can serve to remove the root and the effect of wickedness by promoting repentance and justice.[15]

Augustine, in reference to "wickedness" and "mortality" (*uer. rel.* xi.21),[16] chooses his own equivalent terms calling them "sin" (*peccatum*) and "penalty" (*poena*) and admits that they alone constitute "the entirety which can be called evil" (*totum quod dicitur malum*) (xii.23; xx.39).[17] The term "evil" (*malum*) here is used as referring not to its nature but to the human experience of it. Viewed from the perspective of nature, Augustine can consider "sin" as truly evil, whereas "the penalty of sin" for the promotion of divine justice is inherently good (*Fort.* 15). His consideration that the two terms, originally influenced by the Manichaean categorization of evil, are definitive in range indicates his intention to develop his own ideas of the personal experience of evil along the Manichaean lines. Yet Augustine treats the human experience of evil differently from that of the Manichees on two counts: he rejects determinism and denies the substantiality of evil.

Sin as wickedness redefined.   Since Augustine rejected determinism, his concept of "sin" as wickedness is an expansion of the Manichaean idea of spiritual evil understood as the presence of turbulent desire in the soul. His focus is on the role of the will as the soul's movement in choosing turbulent bodily pleasures instead of tranquil enjoyment of God. Although he would agree with the Manichees that spiritual evil is intrinsic evil, he believes that it is so, not because the soul is *in* the body, but because of the involvement of the moral agency of the soul in voluntary defection (*uer. rel.* xiv.27–28). This point is well captured in the following passage:

> No life is evil as life except as it tends to death. Indeed, in regard to life, death is but wickedness, which is derived from what may be called "nothingness." And, therefore, wicked men are called men of nothing. Hence, life which by voluntary defects turns away from him who made it, whose essence it enjoyed, and, against God's law, wants to enjoy bodily objects over which God put it in charge, tends to nothingness. This is wickedness, but not because the body as such is nothing.[18]

In subsequent discussions, we must understand that the mention of the enjoyment of corporeal objects has all the ramifications of carnal pleasure brought about by loving those objects. This may be hinted at by Augustine's (possibly intentional) ambiguity in his use of the term *corpus* to refer to the human body as well as to corporeal objects loved by the soul for the sake of giving pleasure to the human body. This intentional ambiguity becomes evident when we study the possibility of the meaning of *corpus* and its derivatives in the whole context of *uer. rel.* xi.22–xii.23. For example, in saying that life which enjoys bodily delights (*corporis delectata*) neglects God, Augustine could easily shift the meaning from delight in physical objects to the implication of pleasures experienced by the body that are generated by the love of these objects. Thus, regarding the reversal of the voluntary defection, we are admonished to turn our love "from bodily pleasure to the eternal essence of truth" (*a corporis uoluptatibus ad aeternam essentiam ueritatis*) (i.e., God), where the pleasure (*uoluptas*) is excessive (*in copia*) and needs to be restrained by temperance (xv.29).

Penalty as mortality redefined. Augustine follows the Neoplatonic tradition and asserts that the nature of evil is simply corruption of the Good. He wants to answer the question of "What is evil?" which is posed in *mor.* II.ii.2. To him, the defective turning of the will would definitely be a kind of corruption or what he later calls "voluntary corruption" (*uoluntaria corruptio*), but more insightful from the consideration of Manichaean influence is "penal corruption" (*poenalis corruptio*) in his explanation of mortality as the penalty of sin (*fund.* xxxix.45). The Manichaean concept of mortality as physical evil, according to Augustine, would mean the harm, and ultimately death, suffered by the body. He takes up this Manichaean idea of bodily harm but reinterprets it to mean corruption of the body due to sudden loss of well-being that results in grief. Nevertheless, as penalty for sin, the grief suffered does not remain only with the body, but also affects the soul:[19]

> For loving inferior things, [a human being] is given over to punishment.
> It is oriented toward hell, deprived of its pleasures and in grief. What is
> the grief of the body except the sudden corruption of salvation of the
> thing which the soul by using badly has subjected it to corruption? And
> what is the grief of the soul but to miss the mutable things which the
> soul enjoyed or hoped to be able to enjoy?[20]

This extension of the Manichaean concept of mortality from the perspective of human fallenness,[21] as we will see later, has definitive consequences in Augustine's own formulation of an alternative explication for the inevitability of personal evil.[22] In the above quotation alone, other than both being consequent upon sin (*peccatum*), we do not seem to have yet observed a direct causal connection between grief of the body and grief of the soul. Yet, in the ensuing paragraphs, we are told that the corrupted body may be restored to its original pristine stability if the soul reverts from enjoying carnal pleasure to enjoying God who gives stability (xii.25). Hence, there is assumed a causal relation in the direction from soul to body in terms of maintaining the integrity of a human person.

But even more interesting is to look for the reverse causal relation from body to soul in the sense of how the corrupted body affects the soul. Augustine habitually quotes from Wis. 9:15: "corrupted body weighs down the soul" (*corpus, quod corrumpitur, aggrauat animam*) (xxi.41). This burdened soul becomes the reason for moral difficulty, the just penalty of sin or vice (xx.39). Augustine is struggling here for an answer whose development we now trace.

Since Augustine considers both angels and humans to be rational beings, his views on the former will lead us to his understanding of the human condition. Augustine opines that the evil of the fallen angels lay in their turning away from God to the love of self in pride:

> With their will, by loving God rather than themselves, they [good angels] remain firm and stable in him and enjoy his majesty, being gladly subject to him alone. But that angel by loving himself more than God, did not want to be subject to him [God]. Swelling with pride, he defected from the supreme essence and fell. Owing to this, he is less than what he was, because he wanted to enjoy that which was less, in wishing to enjoy his own power rather than God's. Although he was not supremely, he was more amply when he enjoyed that which is supremely, for God alone supremely is. Indeed, whatever is less than what it was, is evil not insofar as it is but insofar as it is less. For inasmuch as it is less than what it was, it tends toward death. What is strange about defect coming from poverty and out of poverty envy, because of which the Devil is the Devil.[23]

As for the Devil, the lower thing he turns to is self by way of self-love, his lesser state is poverty (*inopia*), and his vicious turn against God envy. But is it not true that envy is not only caused by self-love but is in fact a manifestation of self-love? Thus, because of self-love, the Devil is made less (the essential meaning of corruption). Yet, out of this corrupt condition, he is even more desirous of self-love. In the cited passage, the last remark about envy as the defining character of the Devil may then be perceived as Augustine's recognition that the crux of the problem of evil is in its *ever deepening vicious spiral*, an inherent mechanism in his notion of *consuetudo*.

From the description of the Devil, we note a parallel situation with fallen human beings: both turn away from God for something lower, both are less than what they originally were, and both in the lesser state turn even more against God. Therefore, although the wicked angel tempted humans, however, they consented to defect from God (xiv.27–28). In terms of human corruption, Augustine is careful to raise the issue of human corporeality: the human body was perfect prior to sin, and only afterward has it become weak and mortal. In this state, love of bodily pleasures becomes the height of the problem that needs to be corrected (*uer. rel.* xv.29).

As with pride in the Devil, fallen humanity remains in its present predicament because of self-love. It is self-love expressed through human corporeality in the form of pursuing bodily pleasures by means of loving physical objects (*corpus*). In the corrupt state, the human body in its weakness and mortality burdens the soul, which is made susceptible to the deceptively sweet appeal of such pleasures (xv.29). This is the penal condition experienced by the soul of a fallen human: the mutable thing loved puts one in misery by feeding the soul with deceptive pleasures (*fallaces uoluptates*) which are transitory and do not satisfy (xx.40). This is Augustine's proposal for the reverse causal relation of how the corrupt body affects the soul.

The consequence of the voluntary defection is not only moral difficulty but also epistemic ignorance of the truth in unity. This situation of double jeopardy is well captured by the second half of Augustine's quote from Wis. 9:15: "corrupted body weighs down the soul and the earthly tent burdens the thoughtful mind" (*corpus, quod corrumpitur, aggrauat animam et deprimit terrena inhabitatio sensum multa cogitantem*) (xxi.41; cf. *Gen. Man.* II.xx.30). These two aspects of ignorance and moral difficulty do not just run parallel to each other. In the deception afforded by the mutable things mentioned earlier, Augustine wants to imply that the problem of moral difficulty is in part due to ignorance. The reason why one is deceived into deriving pleasure from corporeal objects is, at least partly, because of one's inability to see through the multiplicity of these mutable things to the unity of the eternal God. Thus, the pursuit of the many mutable objects becomes the only option for a carnal person. G.R. Evans attributes Augustine's association of evil (or carnality) and matter (or corporeal objects) in his epistemology to the lingering influence of Manichaeism.[24] The issue at stake is no simple matter:

> The variety of temporal appearance has through carnal senses, diverted fallen humanity from the unity of God, and multiplied its affectivity in changeable variety. So has abundance been made laborious, and, if one may say so, need made abundant, as long as it pursues one thing after another, and nothing truly remains with it.[25]

Moreover, Augustine points out that, in the absence of divine providence, one will experience strong reaction when one tries to resist the flesh and transcend the appearances of mutable objects. When one stretches the physical senses to make them do the impossible task of spiritual contemplation,[26] the result will be the more serious error of arriving at phantasms because the real problem of carnal mindedness is not solved (xx.40). Augustine claims that the Manichees' worship of phantasms is worse than the pagan's idolatry because the idol is at least made of real matter (*Faus.* XX.5; *uer. rel.* xxxviii.69). In this claim, he seems to feel that the key problem of the struggle of the flesh resides in the mind. But what is the true nature of this "flesh"—the principle of personal evil—that Augustine has only implicitly assumed in the foregoing discussion? And is there a mechanism by which the flesh plays out its role? We will answer both questions simultaneously.

Alternative explanation of personal evil. If it is true that Augustine's concept of human experience of evil is an adaptation of its Manichaean counterpart (disturbance of tranquil pleasure), we must add that through this adaptation he has at this point basically succeeded also in retaining the Manichaean insight of the inevitability of personal evil (as we will see below), by introducing a vicious circle of cause and effect regarding the fallen human condition of existence. It is evident that the preceding discourse reflects Augustine's conscious effort to seek an alternative explanation of the phenomenon of what the Manichees believe to be caused by a metaphysical evil principle (xxiii.44), and only in *De uera religione* has he embarked on developing a full theory.

By renaming "wickedness" and "mortality" as "sin" and "punishment," Augustine has imposed a causal relation on the two Manichaean terms. As such, mortality is consequential to wickedness. Augustine tries to justify this causal link by resorting to an etymological derivation of "wickedness" (*nequitia*) from "nothingness" (*ne quidquam*), a term easily associated with death or mortality in the context of life (xi.21). This understanding of "wickedness" reminds us of his early etymological exercise in *De beata uita* (ii.8) where he opposes *nequitia* to *frugalitas*,[27] the key to his concept of fullness of existence. If life may be understood as fullness of existence, then death would be the lack of existence to the point of arriving at nothingness.

Moreover, Augustine's augmentation of the Manichaean idea of "mortality" has provided a needed structural extension for the formation of a vicious circle. Thus, wickedness of the soul causes harm to the body but the harmed body in turn burdens the soul. To close the circle, Augustine only needs to find a common link between the role of the soul at the first stage and its role at the last. And this missing link is bodily pleasure, which provides the driving force for the vicious circle. From the perspective of the influence of the Manichaean notion of "wickedness" as turbulent pleasure, we observe here that Augustine in the process of closing the circle subsumes under that notion both the soul's susceptibility as well as its voluntary defection to that pleasure.[28]

To summarize, the vicious circle begins as the soul voluntarily defects toward bodily pleasure. This defection causes bodily corruption that burdens the soul with increased susceptibility to the appeal of further bodily pleasure. The dynamic notion of turbulence inherent in the Manichaean idea of bodily pleasure is now put to work in this mechanism of a vicious circle. Moreover, the blinding effect due to ignorance is an added assurance of bondage to this pleasure. There is then no need for the supposition of a substantial evil principle to work behind the scenes in a person, because the enticement of the bodily pleasure with its blinding effect on the soul is enough to keep a fallen human in perpetual bondage. In the absence of divine grace, the human existential condition of "corruption" provides an alternative explanation to the phenomenon of human inner struggle.[29] Or in other words, the "flesh" as an evil principle is this corruptive condition, characterized by the soul's earthly affection, being sustained in the mortal body. *Consuetudo*, then, is the corruptive condition—or the flesh—played out in the vicious circle mechanism, from which comes the mysterious gravitation toward evil. A little later, Augustine would ascertain that even though it is not a true metaphysical evil nature as the Manichees would assert, this "habit of sinners" (*consuetudo peccatorum*) has nevertheless "turned into a natural state" (*in naturam uersa*) (*fid. sym.* x.23).

Affirmation in Subsequent Works

After *De uera religione*, there are many references to *consuetudo* but two examples will suffice to demonstrate the continuity of ideas. In *De duabus animabus*, there is only a short reference to *consuetudo* but it is enough to indicate the assumption of the developed theory:

> For it is not without penalty that by the sin of transgression we have been turned from immortal to mortal beings. So it happens, that when we strive for better things, habit formed with the flesh and our sins somehow began to war against us and to give us difficulty [...].[30]

We note here that there is no more mention of "mystery" about the effect of mortality because the mystery has already been solved in *De uera religione* (cf. *Gen. Man.* II.xix.29). Also, *consuetudo* is now qualified as something produced with the flesh (*facta cum carne*). Although this expression is first coined in *De musica* VI.xi.33 (391), the present idea can be traced back to *De uera religione*, as shown in the preceding discussion concerning the relation between the flesh as corruptive condition and *consuetudo*.[31] In fact, taking into account that the same coined expression is repeatedly used in *Contra Fortunatum* 22, we might suggest that possibly its employment in *De duabus animabus* presupposes at least some of the ramifications in the later elaboration, when Augustine is then forced to explain and clarify himself under the pressure of the debate with Fortunatus. Indeed, the long-sought explicit link between *consuetudo* and the notion of the principle of personal evil is found in *Contra Fortunatum*. In an illustration from swearing, Augustine points out clearly that what some people call "root of evil" (*mali stirps*) is nothing but *consuetudo* (*Fort.* 22), about which he says:

> [...] free choice of the will was present in that man who was the first to be formed. He was made in such a way that nothing at all could have resisted his will, if he had willed to keep the precepts of God. But after he sinned by that free will, we who have descended from his progeny have been plunged into necessity. Each one of us can with a little reflection find that what I say is true. For at present in our actions, before we get entangled by any habit, we have free choice to do or not do something. But when with that freedom we have done something and the destructive sweetness and pleasure of that deed has taken hold of the soul, by the very same habit the soul is so entangled that afterwards it cannot overcome that [habit] which it has forged for itself by sinning.[32]

Three important points in this passage reflect the theory previously developed. First, it tells us that the primal sin causes us to be in the present predicament of the inevitability of personal evil by taking from us freedom of choice. Then, it explains that the lack of freedom is due to a vicious *consuetudo* that entangles us once we are in it. And the key to its binding force is the enticement of sweetness and pleasure. Moreover, we are told that this *consuetudo* which wars against the soul is considered the mind of the flesh until the mind is illuminated by God. Thus, Augustine believes that the mind holds the key to one's release from carnality by letting in the divine light of truth, as is supposed in *De uera religione* (xx.40).[33]

It has been asserted that the idea of *consuetudo* in *duab. anim.* xiii.19 refers to "the inability to control the body which is a natural and involuntary consequence of mortality" and hence must be distinguished from "the customs established by voluntary consent" mentioned in *Fort.* 22.[34] Yet, careful reading shows that there is no such difference in meaning between the two passages; instead, there is a clarification of the earlier work in the later. In the public debate with Fortunatus, Augustine is forced to expand and systematize his view expressed in *De duabus animabus* through a re-interpretation of the Pauline texts cited by his Manichaean opponent.[35] Public debate with the Manichees forces Augustine to "construct a synthetic, as well as a polemical, reading of the Apostle" in dealing with the issue of sin and hence incites him to work on the Pauline commentaries.[36] This view may be supported by Augustine's mention of the carnal mind's inability to subject itself to the law of God, a theme more thoroughly developed in his subsequent writings that deal with the issue raised in the Letter to the Romans.[37] This being said, we must not overlook the fact that the content of Augustine's systematization on the notion of *consuetudo* is already found in *De uera religione*, although there could be a clarification of ideas along the Pauline route. Hence, it is suggested that Augustine for the first time gives *consuetudo* "the force of necessity" in his debate with Fortunatus, and, consequently, from now on he has to restrict the exercise of free will to the first human.[38] But the implication of this "force" has already been in place in the vicious circle mechanism developed earlier.

The Concept of *Concupiscentia*

Augustine's pejorative notion of *concupiscentia* is intimately linked to *consuetudo*, and has occupied his attention in subsequent thinking. In the writings leading to his mature view of grace and after, he refers at times to the two concepts interchangeably (*doc. chr.* I.xxiv.24–25). In the following study of the Manichaean influence of Augustine's idea of *concupiscentia*, we will try to address three issues: 1) whether there is a direct link between the Manichaean notion of evil and Augustine's concept of *concupiscentia*, 2) the role of *concupiscentia* in the notion of *consuetudo*, which has been argued to be influenced by the Manichaean notion of evil as wickedness and mortality, and 3) the continuity in the notion of *concupiscentia* before and after Augustine's focus on the Pauline text.

Direct Link from the Manichaean Idea of Evil

In recent years, van Oort has succeeded in identifying a close parallel between the Manichaean notion of evil matter as random motion within an individual and Augustine's concept of "uncontrollable impulse" (*motus inmoderatus*) in human disposition. Yet, van Oort refrains from concluding that Augustine borrows directly from the Manichees. Tracing the historical influence to both Mani and Augustine, he is only willing to concede the possibility of a common root between the two views.[39] But we would show in two stages that Augustine's notion of *concupiscentia* indeed comes from his understanding of the Manichaean doctrine of evil. First, we will show that there is a link between Augustine's understanding of this notion in Manichaeism and his general usage. Second, we will show that Augustine acquires the strong sexual overtone he gives to *concupiscentia* from the Manichaean understanding of the term.

Existence of the link.   The classical use of the term *concupiscentia* gives it a general meaning of longing or desire, without a necessarily pejorative implication.[40] This point may be reflected in Augustine's citation of the Latin translation of Wis. 6:12–20 in *mor.* I.xvii.32, where we are told that the beginning of wisdom is the *concupiscentia* of discipline, and that the *concupiscentia* of wisdom brings us to God's kingdom. Here, the meaning of the term intended by the translator is certainly positive. But in various usages outside the writings of Augustine, *concupiscentia* has the connotation of inordinateness.[41] We find that he adopts this pejorative connotation as his basic understanding of *concupiscentia* for that reflects the Manichaean idea of evil as turbulence.

As we have shown earlier, the Manichaean notion of the Good is the Beautiful that engenders tranquil pleasure, and evil is whatever disturbs that pleasure. In his recounting of the writing of *De pulchro et apto*, Augustine identifies this disturbance as including shameful *libido* (*conf.* IV.xv.24).[42] That the strong sexual overtone of this term is characteristically the concern of the Manichees may be further illustrated by Augustine's early reference to *what the Manichees say* about their moral symbol of the breast: it is said to be for the purpose of checking all the potential tendencies of *libido* (*mor.* II.x.19). From his remarks on the Manichaean myth about recovering the light particles from the powers of darkness, we perceive that, according to Augustine's understanding of Manichaeism, *libido* is synonymous with *concupiscentia*. In that myth, Augustine recalls that the powers of light in both sexes are sent by God the Father from his light-ship (the sun) to have intercourse with the adverse powers. In the arousal and relaxation of *concupiscentia* during the process of intercourse, the powers of darkness release the particles (*nat. bon.* xliv; cf. *haer.* xlvi). In fact, when recounting the same myth elsewhere, Augustine mentions the two synonyms side by side as "blazing passion and gaping concupiscence" (*flagrantis libido et inhiantis concupiscentia*) (*Faus.* XX.6).

The above idea of disturbance conceived of in relation to *libido* and *concupiscentia* is not only preserved in Augustine's remarks about Manichaeism, it is also transferred to his general reference to the unruly emotions that burst forth and turn into evil *consuetudo* carrying us off with destructive desire (*delectatio*). These emotions are likened to beasts that need to be tamed by reason. It is noteworthy, nonetheless, that Augustine shows the background of this specific notion of disturbance to be in Paul's Gal. 5:24: "For whoever belong to Jesus Christ have crucified their flesh with disturbance and concupiscence" (*Qui autem Iesu Christi sunt, carnem suam crucifixerunt cum perturbationibus et concupiscentiis*) (*Gen. Man.* I.xx.31).

Besides the direct link between Augustine's notion of *concupiscentia* and his understanding of Manichaeism, there is also supporting evidence of this connection in his use of the term in anti-Manichaean polemic. As his common practice, he tries to employ the Manichaean concepts to fight the Manichees.[43] Thus, if Augustine accuses his opponents of being concupiscent, then it would mean that he has invested, at least in part, a Manichaean meaning into the term *concupiscentia*; otherwise, he would not get the point across because the term would not mean for them what it means to him.

Augustine's notion of *concupiscentia* does not restrict itself to the sexual realm,[44] but is also applied generally to mean uncontrolled desire, such as excessive appetite in eating. This latter point is what he finds fault with the Manichees. In *mor.* II.xvi.51, he accuses them of promoting *concupiscentia* in eating because the Manichees, while condemning those who consume animal flesh even without *concupiscentia*, encourage others to eat food other than animal flesh though with excessive appetite.[45]

The Manichaean prohibition of consuming animal flesh is based on their belief that the flesh of dead animals is utterly filthy, for it is formed from the residual dregs after divine elements have escaped in various ways (*mor.* II.xv.37; *haer.* xlvi). On the other hand, the encouragement of the elect to eat plant food is due to the other aspect of the same Manichaean doctrine. The Manichees believe, as understood by Augustine, that the divine substance is being daily released. In its passage upward as vapor from earth to heaven, it enters plants whose roots are fixed in the earth. But the divine substance contained in the plants can only be returned to the domain of light by the purification process of the elect's mastication and digestion (*mor.* II.xv.36; *conf.* III.x.18; *nat. bon.* xlv; *ennar.* CXL.6). In view of this doctrine, the underlying logic in Augustine's polemic is understandably to refute the Manichaean moral inconsistency. The cruelty of forbidding animal flesh when it might be needed for health reasons contradicts the seemingly good principle of preventing one from defilement. But more, the good moral behavior of the elect in releasing the light particles through mastication and digestion is more than offset by their evil *concupiscentia* in eating.

On this last point, Augustine must have assumed that his Manichaean readers knew exactly what *concupiscentia* meant in order for his refutation to have made sense. And obviously, the Manichaean notion of the term is "excessive appetite." Again, we can also find a Pauline connection to this concept. In his response to the Manichaean question about the Apostle's exhortation not to eat flesh, Augustine quotes Paul (Rom. 13:14) to mean not to indulge in *concupiscentia* in regard to eating (*mor.* II.xiv.31). This avoidance of *concupiscentia* for food, as Augustine defends the high moral standard of the Church, is practiced by the Catholic ascetics (*mor.* I.xxxi.67) in view of abstaining from *concupiscentia* in general (xxxiii.71). We see the same idea of *concupiscentia* being applied here to both the Manichaean understanding as well as the non-Manichaean usage (though with the concern of defending the Church against Manichaeism). Thus, we have shown that at least in the general understanding of *concupiscentia* as inordinate desire, Augustine has assumed in the term the Manichaean idea of evil as loss of tranquility, but this assumption is not without the control of Pauline reference. Does Augustine's understanding of *concupiscentia* faithfully reflect that of Paul? Or, put it differently, has he further modified Paul's meaning to fit the Manichaean idea of evil?

The Manichaean sexual overtone.   We will show that there is a change of emphasis in the concept of *concupiscentia* early around 388 when Augustine consciously attempts to equate the term with *libido*. In the process, *concupiscentia* has acquired a strong sexual overtone although he has never forsaken its more general understanding.

We can identify at least two such instances. The first occurs in *lib. arb.* I (iii.8–iv.10), where in the course of looking for an alternative explanation for the root cause of evil deeds,[46] he identifies it to be *libido*. But immediately, he equates *libido* with lust (*cupiditas*), a term (linked etymologically to *concupiscentia*) Augustine has just identified (*mor.* I.xix.35) in the Pauline reference of 1 Tim. 6:10: "lust is the root of all evils" (*radix omnium malorum cupiditas*). Judged from the context of the verse, which is about avarice, *cupiditas* does not have any sexual implications. Yet, in two years' time, the same term has acquired a strong sexual overtone in Augustine's usage (*uer. rel.* xli.78). His second attempt to equate *libido* with *concupiscentia* has already been mentioned above in reference to *Gen. Man.* I.xx.31.[47] There, *libido* is synonymous with *concupiscentia*. The cited Gal. 5:24, when the context is taken into account, again does not particularly refer to sexual passion *per se*. And even in his own remarks preceding the citation of the verse, Augustine only discusses general human irrationality. Although, as just illustrated, in the anti-Manichaean critique his predominant use of *concupiscentia* around 388 concerns excessive appetite for food, it is only a short step from there to his emphasis on sexual desire in "concupiscence of the flesh" (*concupiscentia carnis*) (*uer. rel.* xxvi.48, xxxviii.69).

Therefore, by 390 when *De uera religione* was composed, Augustine has completed the transfer of the Manichaean notion of *libido* to *concupiscentia*. (This has once more proved the significance of this work in Augustine's development of the idea of evil.) In the formulation of an alternative theory to explain the root (*radix*) of evil, he borrows from the Manichaean notion of *libido* but only at the level of human experience, while leaving himself open to substitute the Manichaean notion of a substantial evil principle by his philosophical speculation of *consuetudo* as well as the subsequent Pauline emphasis of *concupiscentia* as an intrinsic rebellious principle.

Central Role of *Concupiscentia* in *Consuetudo*

Although the text where the theory of personal evil is developed in *De uera religione* has only one mention of the term "concupiscence of the eyes" (*concupiscentia oculorum*), in the sense of curiosity (xx.40), it establishes a link to the other aspects in Augustine's comments on 1 Jn. 2:16: "Do not love the world for those which are in the world are concupiscence of the flesh, concupiscence of the eyes and ambition of the world" (*Nolite diligere mundum, quoniam ea, quae in mundo sunt, concupiscentia carnis est et concupiscentia oculorum et ambitio saeculi*).[48] The centrality of this verse in the work may be inferred from Augustine's repeated reference or allusion to it, which occurs near both the beginning (iii.4) and the end of the work as an exhortation to Romanianus (lv.107).

The most interesting reference, however, is the middle one where Augustine equates concupiscence of the flesh (*concupiscentia carnis*) with love of debased pleasure (*uoluptas infima*), concupiscence of the eyes (*concupiscentia oculorum*) with curiosity, and ambition of this world with pride (*superbia*) (xxxviii.70). In his explanation of the operational relationship between these three terms, he summarizes the gist of the theory of personal evil we saw earlier: bondage comes as one's pride leads to self-love in the form of the pursuit of carnal delights, and one's curiosity adds to the viciousness of the situation by deceiving the soul into thinking that there is no other alternative (i.e., worshipping God as the highest truth) (xxxviii.69). Under general consideration, *concupiscentia* is the force that keeps one in bondage. Although the blinding effect of *concupiscentia oculorum* helps the enticement of *uoluptas* or *concupiscentia carnis* to work (xx.40), it seems that it is the enticing sweetness (*dulcedo*) of the latter that does the more serious damage by drawing one back to sin repeatedly (xv.29), and hence, as the logic goes, enables *consuetudo* to entrench.

This last point, if not already made clear in *De uera religione*, is attested in *Contra Fortunatum*, where Augustine asserts that it is the "pernicious sweetness and pleasure" (*perniciosa dulcedo et uoluptas*) of the deed that render a person unable to overcome the habit formed (22). In *De sermone domini in monte* I (393/394), he explicitly suggests that *consuetudo* is the means by which *carnalis delectatio* or carnal desire can operate in us to take us captive (xii.36). This suggestion sets the general tone for Augustine's subsequent idea regarding the relationship between *consuetudo* and *concupiscentia carnalis*: *consuetudo*, on the one hand, serves as a means to realize in behavior the bondage imposed on us by *concupiscentia*, and on the other hand, enforces such a bondage by the process of entrenchment (*Simpl.* I.i.11; *conf.* VI.xii.22; *Iul.* II.iii.5; VI.xviii.55; cf. *ser. dom.* I.xii.36). From this consideration, *concupiscentia* is part of the general picture of *consuetudo*; but it is the part so fundamental from the standpoint of personal evil, that Augustine gradually shifts his attention from the latter to the former.

Continuity of the Notion of *Concupiscentia*

That Augustine's early concept of *concupiscentia* underwent an evolution due to the Manichaean notion of *libido* does not deny that his more general understanding of *concupiscentia* as uncontrolled desire for worldly things is always in use, which is also a result of the influence from the Manichaean concept of evil as loss of tranquility. At the point when the full theory of *consuetudo* is developed, *concupiscentia* becomes only a part of the total picture. After his new attention to the Pauline writings, however, it seems that Augustine is inspired to return to the issue of intrinsic rebellion in human existence, an issue which may not be satisfactorily answered by the postulation of the vicious circle mechanism of *consuetudo* without resorting to focusing on *concupiscentia* as the very root of the problem. This shift is well noted by Babcock as occurring in the debate with Fortunatus when Augustine is brought face to face with the Pauline question of inner struggle.[49] That may explain why only in *Fort.* 22 can we find an explicit reference to the enslaving function of the sweetness of pleasures (cf. *concupiscentia*), even though the idea might already be at hand in *De uera religione*. The reason could be that in the latter the overarching Johannine notion of *concupiscentia* may not have brought out the issue of inner struggle as forcefully as Paul does. Hence, without forsaking either the theory of *consuetudo* or the Manichaean insight of evil as the negation of tranquil pleasure, Augustine gradually relies more on invoking the authority of Paul to explain the problem of personal evil in terms of *concupiscentia carnalis*.

Whether it is the notion of *consuetudo* or *concupiscentia*, we have shown Augustine to be a master artificer in turning the relatively simplistic Manichaean concepts into rich ideas that defend the Christian faith, yet, at the same time, preserve the Manichaean insights. As we will see, the concept of the inevitability of personal evil is fundamental to the development of his doctrine of predestination. From this consideration, we may say that Manichaeism has contributed to the doctrine by drawing Augustine to wrestle with the issue of the evil principle in the context of the Manichaean concept of the Good as the Beautiful.

CHAPTER FIVE

DOCTRINE OF PREDESTINATION

Supreme Good: The Foundational Context

In Augustine's mature notion in *Ad Simplicianum*, we understand him to mean that God's gracious but hidden election predetermines the salvation or damnation of each one belonging to the *massa damnata*. While others are left alone, God's prevenient grace prepares for the faith of the elect to respond favorably to the divine calling. There are two identifiable issues involved in the question of the Manichaean influence; that is, the hiddenness of God's gracious election and the inevitability of personal evil. But these notions must be understood within the context of the cosmic order, which is deemed beautiful. This is Augustine's address to the Manichaean dualistic view of the universe. As his idea of personal evil (already shown to be an adaptation of Manichaean ideas) matures, it also forces a change in the conceptual framework of this cosmic order, a change that reflects the notion of hiddenness of divine election. Yet behind God's hidden election of individuals from the *massa damnata*, there lies the presupposition that God is the Supreme Good considered both in eschatological and cosmic aspects.

The Eschatological Aspect

In some studies of Augustine's doctrine of predestination, attention has often been exclusively focused on the issue of determinism.[1] This focus overlooks the doctrine's eschatological context. At the heart of the matter, it is not just *how* an individual is chosen but *for what* one is chosen. This aspect, although only implicitly assumed in *Ad Simplicianum* I (e.g., ii.6), is brought out as the climax of the last book of *Confessiones* where the issue of predestination is treated in Augustine's confession as an ascent to God. Thus, in one of his final prayers, Augustine asks:

> O Lord God, give us peace—for you have provided us with all things—
> the peace of rest, the peace of the sabbath, the peace without an evening.
> The entire order of things, by the fact that their measures are fulfilled,
> though most beautiful, will pass away. For certainly in them there has
> been a morning, and also an evening.[2]

Put within the immediately preceding context (*conf.* XIII.xxxiv.49), this
passage, couched in the language of creation's six days, is about the
working of God's predestination in one's life on earth from conversion to
faithful service in the Church. But all will be transformed in the final
consummation of the sabbath peace.

In this expectation, Augustine's mention of "peace" (*pax*) suggests
that Supreme Good is a presupposition to the doctrine of predestination.
As shown earlier, the idea that Supreme Good is the guarantor of tranquil
enjoyment reflects the influence of the Manichaean notion of the Good as
the Beautiful that engenders tranquil pleasure. Nevertheless, put in the
eschatological context, the enjoyment of "life-bringing pleasure" (*diliciae
uitales*) (xxi.29) by having one's inner life ordered is no longer subject to
earthly interruption, but is everlasting. If, indeed, what has been
accomplished on earth prior to this eternal sabbath is already called "most
beautiful," and hence engendering much tranquil pleasure, then the
enjoyment of the sabbath peace in God must be beyond comprehension.
Therefore, the whole question of predestination is how, given such a great
Good of eternal peace in God, we are to understand God's gracious
operation in guaranteeing its availability to fallen humankind within the
framework of divine justice.

In considering God's gracious operation, we may perceive an added
dimension of Supreme Good as the guarantor of peace to humanity. From
the perspective of predestination alone, in his initiative to call and to
preveniently prepare the heart of the elect, God assumes an active role to
assure the accomplishment of granting peace. But existence is the
prerequisite to predestination and both are secured in God's gracious
operation. Hence, for Augustine, divine grace is often viewed from two
angles: creation and re-creation, or formation and re-formation. Thus, in
the beginning of *conf.* XIII, Augustine confesses to God: "Out of your
goodness which preceded all that you made me to be and all out of which
you made me" (*ex bonitate tua praeueniente totum hoc, quod me fecisti et
unde me fecisti*) (i.1). On the other hand, God's self-sufficiency also
reflects his passive role as guarantor of peace. Since he is not subject to
vicissitude, he is the sure ground on which we can rely without fear of loss
of peace. Also, Augustine confesses that it is not because of God's need

that he creates and re-creates us but because we need him and only with him may we be well (i.1). God is the ground of peace by reason of his supreme existence, by which *grace* is only a manifestation of his inner richness or *plenitudo bonitatis* (ii.2, iv.5). Indeed, then, grace would be reminiscent of Augustine's early concept of *frugalitas*.

The Cosmic Aspect

In his supreme existence, however, God is also the guarantor of order expressed in both the act of creating and the role of governing, so that the Good or the beauty of the universe may be preserved in harmony. In the act of creating, God as the Supreme Good brings the universe into existence *ex nihilo* by giving *forma* to both corporeal and spiritual beings (ii.2–3). In governing, God puts things in their proper places as illustrated by Augustine's allegorical understanding of the separation between sea and the dry land (xvii.20–21). Here, God has set the limit for the sea that the land may have a chance to germinate life. Interpreted from the view of predestination, the *massa damnata*[3] whose lust is symbolized by the unruliness of the sea is being contained in order that life may grow in the elect, which is prefigured by "the dry land." The notion of cosmic order is actually the framework of Augustine's doctrine of predestination, and is his response to the Manichaean view of the universe as a mixture of good and evil.

Order: The Framework

The Structure of the Framework

That "order" is the framework of the developing doctrine of predestination first becomes evident in *De moribus Manichaeorum* where Augustine discusses the relation between order and existence. Augustine equates the two for the case of creaturely existence:

> Indeed, things which tend toward being tend toward order, and when they have attained the latter they attain being itself, in so far as a creature can attain it. For order reduces that which it orders to a certain conformity [to oneness]; indeed to be is nothing other than to be one. Therefore, in so far as anything acquires unity, to that extent it exists. Truly, conformity and harmony are the working of unity, by which things that are composite exist inasfar as they exist; for simple things exist by themselves since they are one. But things that are not simple imitate unity by the harmony of their parts; and they exist to the extent that they attain it. Wherefore, orderly arrangement brings about being, and disorderly arrangement non-being, which is also called perversion or corruption.[4]

From the context of this cited passage, it is clear that Augustine's discussion has in mind the order of the created universe as a compounded entity. Essential to its existence is therefore unity, which is reflected in the harmony of orderly arrangement of all the individual constituent components. Although endowed by God's supreme existence (*summe esse*), creaturely existence is corruptible and tends to non-existence. Nevertheless, this tendency is reversible, presumably, with the help of the supreme existence. It is curious that just prior to the cited passage Augustine twice mentions the possibility of being changed for the better (*muti in melius*) in the case of already corrupted things as if he wants to set the stage for the subsequent discussion regarding the restoration of the universe.

Immediately following, Augustine tells us that God will arrest the cosmic trend of corruption by judging and then restoring:

> But the goodness of God does not allow matter to be brought to this end [i.e., corruption], but so orders all defective things that they may be at the place where they could exist most suitably, until by their appointed movements they may return to that from which they were defective. Therefore, certainly, when rational souls in whom there is the highest degree of freedom of choice fall away from God, he ranks them among the lower grades of creation, where they are supposed to be. So by divine judgment they suffer misery, yet they are ranked suitably according to what they deserve.[5]

Whether it is judgment or restoration, Augustine's concern is to affirm the initiative of God, the supreme existence, to preserve the existence of the universe by maintaining its proper order. Moreover, Augustine distinguishes two levels of order, the general level of physical existence and the higher moral level that involves only rational beings with the endowment of free will; as such, these beings are capable of moral evil by choosing to defect from God. This hypothesis of a two-tiered structure of universal order is confirmed by Augustine's interpretation of Isa. 45:7, which says: "I make good and create evil" (*Ego facio bona et creo mala*). He understands the first half to refer to the creative act and the second half to the placing of individual evil things in their proper places (vii.9). At the moral level, then, to maintain the existence of the universe would mean administering punishment to sinners, or, to put it differently, sinners are assigned a lower order of existence which is characterized by misery.[6] Considering the hierarchy in creation, however, Augustine would later affirm that even evil rational beings are ranked higher than the highest among the physical objects (*duab. anim.* vi.8).

Fortunately, judgment is not the final story for the existence of the universe. In the anticipation of future restoration, Augustine points out that the will which leads rational beings into corruption in the first place is also "the gate" (*ianua*) of hope that may lead them back to the original state of peace bestowed by God, as is well illustrated by Augustine's citation from Lk: 2:14: "Glory to God in the highest and on earth peace to men of good will" (*Gloria in excelsis deo et in terra pax hominibus bonae uoluntatis*) (vii.10).

A Response to Manichaeism

Indeed, the question of divine judgment and its parallel concerning creation are Augustine's response to the Manichaean view of the mixed presence of good and evil, in both spiritual and physical aspects, in the universe. This assumption of the double aspect is justified by Augustine's two subsequent lengthy critiques of the inconsistency of the Manichaean belief regarding the evil spiritual realm (ix.14–18) as well as the admixture of good and evil elements in the physical world (xvi.38–53). Furthermore, his intention to address the Manichaean view of good and evil is confirmed in his own words to the Manichees:

> It is enough [...] for you to see that there is no way out in the religious disputation regarding good and evil, unless [it is agreed that] whatever is, as far as it is, is from God; however, as far as it lacks essence it is not from God, but, all the same, it is always ordered by divine providence as is fitting to the whole system.[7]

The same concern of Augustine is already expressed in his *De ordine* (386). To this we must return later. For now, let us put this concern into perspective by briefly reviewing the Manichaean myth which explains the presence of good and evil.

Manichaean myth. Manichaeism, as understood by Augustine, seeks to answer the question *unde sit malum?* (Whence comes evil?) (*mor.* II.ii.2) and arrives at a dualistic solution reflected in its cosmogony which is constituted in three Moments: the pristine universe, the present world order, and the eschatological restoration.[8] Of the three, however, only the first two regarding, respectively, the spiritual and the physical aspect of the universe, need concern us here.

In the pristine universe, the two kingdoms of good and evil divided by a border. According to Augustine's quote from the *Epistula Fundamenti*, the Manichees affirm that God the Father, who is self-existent, virtuous and true, rules the kingdom (*imperium*) of light, consisting of twelve divisions (*membra*) which hold untold treasures as well as numerous happy and glorious worlds (*saecula*) united to himself. These magnificient realms of "light and bliss" where the Father resides can never be shaken or disturbed (*fund.* xiii).

On the other side of the border is the kingdom of darkness, a region extending downward in boundless depth and length, having the five caverns of the elements full of darkness, water, wind, fire, and smoke in which dwell the serpents, swimming creatures, flying creatures, quadrupeds, and bipeds, respectively (*mor.* II.ix.17; *fund.* xv, xxviii). All bodies are derived from this region of darkness (*fund.* xxi; *Faus. XX.12*). The first bodies of the princes of darkness are said to be generated like worms from the trees of darkness, trees produced from the five elements (*Faus.* VI.8; *haer.* xlvi). Belonging to this evil kingdom, however, are not just mortal bodies but also malignant spirits (*nat. bon.* ii; cf. *Gen. Man.* I.iv.7). As the Manichees teach that God is the principle of all good things, they also teach that *Hylè*, a formative mind (*mens formatrix*: *Faus.* XX.14), is the principle of evil which gives form to bodies (*Faus.* XX.3).

In the present order, as Augustine recounts it, invasion happened when the race of darkness saw the light of the kingdom of light, delighted in it and desired to possess it (*mor.* II.ix.17). The Manichees assert that God is unshakable; yet his realm was faced with the invasion by the nature of darkness (*fund.* xii) unless he could send some excellent divine power to overcome and destroy the advancing enemy (*nat. bon.* xlii; cf. *mor.* II.xii.15). God sent the Primal Human armed with water, fire, winds, air and light to counter the enemies who were also equipped with waters, fire, winds, smoke and darkness (*Faus.* II.3). This Primal Human and his five elements were said to be of the substance of God (XI.3). By altering his elements to please the princes of darkness, the Primal Human succeeded in capturing those of both sexes and he eventually mixed with the race of darkness (II.4; VI.8; XI.3). Out of this mixture, the present cosmos is made (II.5; cf. XIII.18, XX.9) by the Mighty Spirit (XX.9). It consists of eight earths and ten heavens and is upheld by the World-holder who is in turn borne on the shoulders of Atlas (XV.5–6; XX.9; XXXII.19). Fabrication of the world by commingling the good and the evil elements is the only means available to God to subdue the enemies (*uer. rel.* ix.16).

About the details of how various parts of the world come into being, Augustine recalls that the sun is made of good fire and the moon of good water. In contrast to other creations made out of the admixture of the good and bad elements, the sun and the moon are presumably pure lights and they are called vessels or light-ships in order to receive light particles purified by the angels of light (*haer.* xlvi). These two lights are always united to the air in their course. The power of the Son or Christ was believed to reside in the sun and his wisdom in the moon (*Faus.* XX.8). Other heavenly bodies are less pure because they were made of the princes of darkness who were arranged as higher or lower in the various parts of the world depending on the amount of good mixed in them. Among these princes who were used to form heavenly bodies, some were pregnant females, and due to celestial rotation they abortively gave birth to both sexes that fell to the earth to generate all kinds of animal life on the land, in the air and in the sea (*Faus.* VI.8; XXI.12; *mor.* II.ix.18). Despite the admixture of good and evil, the world is still permeated with good nature, for God's members are in it. Thus, the divine nature can be found in all bodies, in all kinds of flesh, and in all seeds of trees, herbs, humans and animals (*nat. bon.* xliv; cf. *mor.* II.xvii.36–37). By the sweetness of the taste, or the fragrance of the smell, but especially by the beauty of appearance, one is able to discern the amount of good held bound in an object (*mor.* II.xvi.39).

Augustine's response. Under the assumption that what is good is primarily reflected in the beauty of the object, whether corporeal as with physical entities or incorporeal as in the case of the kingdom of light, the Manichees arrive at the conclusion that the present universe is a mixture of both good and evil. Augustine, reasoning along similar lines, concludes differently. He argues that an individual creature is good because of the harmonious congruence of its parts, just as the universe is good by reason of its harmonious order (*mor.* II.v.7–ix.18). The whole point is that beauty resides with order that must be apprehended by the intellect, an act of which the Manichees are incapable (xvi.43). Augustine's argument concerning "order" is first set out in *De ordine* and later significantly advanced in *De uera religione*.

In *De ordine*, Augustine's affirmation of the goodness of order is no doubt motivated by the Manichaean question of *unde sit malum?*. This question is interpreted by him as implying that evil is willed by God (*ord.* I.i.1) when *Hylè* is taken to assume the role of an evil God (*Faus.* XXI.4; *nat. bon.* xviii). But since, according to Augustine, God is good and he is the only ground of existence, then how can something evil come out of the good God? In the affirmation of a trinitarian monism,[9] Augustine is faced with the challenge of explaining the total goodness of the universe despite the presence of evil in it.[10] To put it in Manichaean terms, Augustine must show that the universe is wholly beautiful.

In his approach to the notion of "order," Augustine tries to solve a twofold, yet integrated, problem of ontology and epistemology[11] by means of a Ciceronian modification of Plotinus' aesthetic concept of the Good.[12] This solution is succinctly captured by Trygetius' response to Augustine's question whether disorder is included in order. According to Joanne McWilliam, Trygetius is none other than a portrayal of Augustine's earlier self.[13] This theory is supported by Augustine's immediate endorsement of Trygetius' answer, together with confirming illustrations (II.iv.12–13). Even later when Augustine is asked to clarify his position concerning divine governance, he refers back to this model answer (II.vii.21):

> Recalling [the image] of darkness has brought us not a little light, on what was presented by me in a hazy manner. For indeed, the whole life of fools, although it may hardly be consistent and well-ordered by them, nevertheless is necessarily included in the order of things through a divine providence, which would by no means allow it to be disposed, as it were, by the ineffable and eternal law, where it ought not to be. Therefore, anyone considering that life by itself with a narrow mind is turned away, as though repelled by a great foulness. But if he raises the eyes of the mind and widens his scope, he may survey all things at one time, and he will discover nothing which is not ordered nor always distinct and assigned to its own proper place.[14]

The first part of this response addresses the issue whether order can embrace something with no order, such as the life of an unwise person.[15] The answer is a qualified "Yes." Yet, to avoid the apparent contradiction that order can embrace something disorderly, Augustine must have presupposed that "disorderliness," like "darkness," is a non-positive concept.[16] Evil is rendered harmless if seen from the perspective of a divine providence which places individual disorderly things in their proper place in the grand order.

But even if there is order, how do we know that it is good or beautiful? This is dealt with in the second part of the response. Since the basic idea of order is unity, one has to broaden one's horizon until a holistic vision is attained. Thus, if one merely focuses on the parts, one will inevitably lose sight of the Good in the broader picture. This Good is, however, identified in aesthetic terms as beauty of oneness (*unum*) (I.ii.3) manifested in configuration (I.vii.18), an idea of harmony (*congruens*) rooted in the notion of suitability (*aptum*),[17] whether in visual art or music (II.xi.32). Here, we may trace this idea to Augustine's earliest writing, *De pulchro et apto*.

As to the question why the Manichees are not granted the holistic vision, Augustine's answer is clear: It is not the distracted soul which attains this vision, but one who has acquired the habit of withdrawing from the outward sensible things and concentrating on the inner thought (I.i.3–ii.3). This can only be achieved if one is fixed on the happy or blessed life (*beata uita*) of contemplating God (I.viii.24).[18] To Augustine, one may see beauty in this world when one sees the beauty of God. But one can only see God if one's soul has been well disposed and rendered harmonious and beautiful (II.xix.51), through order (I.ix.27) in moral living (II.xix.50) and even reflection on the disciplines of the liberal arts (II.v.14).[19]

While Augustine in *De ordine* develops the philosophical frame of universal ordering, in *De uera religione* he fleshes it out with the biblical notion of salvation. Assuming the two-tiered structure (cf. xi.21), Augustine gives the concept of divine ordering of the human moral world a linear perspective of history and eschatology in his defence against the Manichaean view of the universe. Thus, he asserts that the beauty of the universe is free from all fault because of these three things: damnation of sinners (*damnatio peccatorum*), exercise of the just (*exercitatio iustorum*), perfection of the blessed (*perfectio beatorum*) (xxiii.44). Put into context, this assertion, we realize, is Augustine's concluding statement on his theory of personal evil. There, he finds that the intrinsic evil is one's voluntary defection from God. Other than that, there is no evil in the universe, because when the individual sinner is punished by being put in the appropriate place, sin does not affect the total cosmic order (xxiii.44).

In the incorporation of the linear perspective into divine ordering, the twofold aspect of ontology and epistemology in *De ordine* is here superimposed with the dual category of authority and reason. Under the consideration of authority, Augustine shifts from what was the individual concern of overcoming personal evil to the global outlook of salvation history, or, in his vocabulary, *historia et prophetia* (xxv.46). Here, Augustine distinguishes the seven stages of the unsaved "old humanity" (*uetus homo*) from those of the regenerated "new humanity" (*nouus homo*). The first dispensation is lived out in the desire for temporal things and finally ends in death whereas the second is lived out in progressive spiritual advancement and leads to eternal rest and beatitude (xxvi.48–49). The significance of this distinction in the global context is to introduce the two classes of the elect and the *massa damnata*. Hence, concerning the old and new humanity, Augustine comments:

> No one doubts that these two kinds of life are as follows: One kind is
> old and earthly which a man could lead during his whole life; another is

truly new and heavenly which no one in this life could live, except with
the old. For the new must both begin from itself and continue with the
old until the visible death, although the old becomes weaker as the new
progresses. So, by analogy, the entire humankind, which is like the life
of an individual from the time of Adam till the end of this world, is so
managed under the laws of divine providence that it appears divided
into two classes. In one of these is the multitude of the impious which
bears the image of the earthly man from the beginning to the end of the
world. In the other is the succession of the people devoted to the one
God. [...] The pious people will be raised so that they may transform the
remnants of their "old man" into the new. But the impious people which
has put on the "old man" from the beginning to the end, will be raised to
be cast into the second death.[20]

Elsewhere, Augustine points out that the pious include godly people from
both the Old and New Testament times. The saints from the time of Adam
to John the Baptist lived under a certain kind of righteousness in
anticipation of the new dispensation. Thus, we find referents to all three
categories (mentioned earlier) of what contributes to the cosmic beauty:
damnation of sinners, exercise of the just and perfection of the blessed
(xxiii.46). While the first category refers to the *massa damnata*, the second
and the third point to the elect through all ages.

If by "authority" Augustine introduces the historical dimension into
the divine ordering of the universe, then by "reason" he means for us to
transcend the temporal historical sequence, of which we are a part, in order
that we may be able to grasp the totality or unity of that ordering.
Therefore, he tells us that while it is possible for anyone to comprehend
the unity of a poem, it is quite impossible to understand historical events
for the simple reason that we are still part of that history (xxii.43), unless,
of course, we can by reason ascend from temporal to eternal things
(xxix.52). From the epistemological consideration, Augustine here wants
to introduce the notion of what is known in modern philosophy as the *a
priori* in aesthetic judgment.[21] That is what distinguishes humans from
animals, although both are living things (xxix.53). The essence of
perception of beauty in corporeal objects is the mental judgment according
to the absolute standard of "equality and unity" (*aequalitas et unitas*)
which is independent of space and time (xxx.56). As absolute standard, it
is even above the rational mind that errs occasionally. Nevertheless,
nothing except God's truth, who is the Son, is above the mind (xxxi.57–
58). Therefore, those who can perceive unity in things are able to do so by
the *true* light (xxxiv.64).

Reminiscent of Augustine's earlier admonition in *De ordine* that the soul be rendered harmonious and beautiful, here he requires us to seek unity in the "simplicity of the heart" (*simplicitas cordis*) (xxxv.65). On the other hand, those who, like the Manichees, cannot see the unity are deceived by illusions or phantasms. They are deceived because they abandon the truth for something else that gives worldly pleasure (xxxvi.67–xxxviii.69). So, the solution is to return and conform to the Principle of congruence from whom all other pleasure-engendering agreeable things derive their inner logic (xxxix.72). Only by abiding in the truth will one be renewed by it (xxxix.73), and in so doing, be able to apprehend the order in all the things of this divinely governed universe, including the appreciation of the beauty in the judgment of sinners (xl.76). Therefore, in response to the Manichees' belief that the universe is an admixture of both good and evil, Augustine establishes a two-tiered cosmic framework to explain how the universe as a whole can still be beautiful despite the presence of evil. Now, we will show the second part of the Manichaean influence in terms of the impact of the principle of personal evil on the development of the doctrine. Having argued already that Augustine's notion of the inevitability of evil is inspired by Manichaeism, we would like to correlate the development of this notion with the degree of determinism in Augustine's various formulations of the idea of election.[22] This will be achieved by observing the role of personal free will in the process, the operation of divine grace, and the contribution of both elements to the subsuming of the determination of individual salvation (not only punishment) to the overarching cosmic order.

Principle of Personal Evil: The Change Factor

In attempting this, we divide the period of our investigation into early, transitional, and mature stages. While most of the essential ideas are put in place in the first and the final outcome is realized in the last, the middle stage that spans approximately six or seven years is most interesting because of the development of ideas involved. Hence, we magnify this transitional stage by further subdividing it into three phases. To take the diachronic changes into account, we treat ideas under each relevant work that is put in chronological sequence. But for the treatment of the early stage, in view of the stability of ideas involved and of the shortness of the time span (about one year), we proceed in a synthetic manner.

Early Stage (388)

As we pointed out in the preceding chapter, Augustine very early on has identified the root of evil in humans to be *libido* or *cupiditas* (lust) (*lib.*

arb. I.iv.10), an adaptation, with a Pauline reference, of the Manichaean idea of inordinate desire.[23] Augustine at this time, however, has not yet ascribed the presence of *libido* to the fall because even Adam, prior to sin, fell by it (*mor.* I.xix.35–36). This does not mean that Augustine has not recognized consequences of human fallenness in spiritual ignorance and moral difficulty (*Gen. Man.* II.xix.29–xx.30). Rather, he does not seem to think that the freedom of the human will is hindered by these effects.

This early position of Augustine is understandable in the light of his attempt to distance himself from the Manichaean determinism he criticizes so harshly, that is, that the soul is assigned by God to suffer by being mixed with the advancing evil (*mor.* II.xii.25; *Faus.* XX.17, XXII.22; *Fort.* 7; *nat. bon.* xlii). To clear God's name of injustice in punishing evil persons, Augustine strains to show that one chooses one's course of action freely (*lib. arb.* I.i.1; xi.22–23). He argues that nothing enslaves the soul to *libido*. By reason of good (universal) order, the stronger rationality (*ratio*) must be able to master the weaker irrational *cupiditas* (x.20); therefore, submission to *libido* is the result of one's own "will and free choice" (*uoluntas et liberum arbitrium*) (xi.21). In spite of the observation that we have never been wise from the day of birth,[24] it is always in our power to "will well" to seek what is eternal (xii.24–26). But since the will to embrace this good will is itself good will, the good will cannot possibly be lost involuntarily as other temporal goods would be (xiii.28–29). In other words, this good will is ultimate by virtue of its self-referencing nature.[25] Therefore, at this stage of Augustine's thinking, one is deemed free to turn to God despite one's mortality (I.xiii.19), and grace, if needed, is available to all indiscriminately (I.iii.6).

In view of Augustine's optimism regarding the freedom of human will to turn to God, voluntary aversion must be justly punished to maintain the cosmic order, yet with the hope of restoration upon conversion (*mor.* II.ix.10). According to their just deserts, sinners are assigned proper places within the hierarchy of rational creation, "until by their orderly movements they return to where they fell from" (*donec ordinatis motibus ad id recurrant unde defecerunt*) (*mor.* II.vii.9).[26] Here, Augustine seems to have left open the possibility of universalism—all fallen rational creatures may one day be restored—a view the aged bishop tries hard to erase from his early record (*retr.* I.vii.6).

Transitional Stage (390–396)

In face of the Manichaean challenge, Augustine believes in the freedom of human will. But it is to be seen whether his growing understanding of the effect of the fall will force him to change his mind. If he is convinced of the defects of the human will but still maintains the idea of divine governance, the tendency toward a more predestinarian view is foreseeable.

We may identify three phases of development here. The first phase goes from 390 to 392, the second from 393 to 394, and the third from 395 to 396.

First phase (390–392). Published in 390 shortly before Augustine's ordination as priest of Hippo Regius, *De uera religione* is a work marking a turn in his career. Since this is a treatise anticipated during the Cassiciacum retreat, it has been argued that the content and method of the book reflect the earlier thought, on especially the motif of ascent.[27] This assessment is possibly based on apparent similarities. Nonetheless, despite Augustine's use of a discourse of ascent from *uer. rel.* xxix.52 onwards, his intention is to point out the presence of human perversity which, without the correction of divine grace, will undoubtedly prevent one from seeing God (e.g., xxxiii.62). Augustine claims from the beginning that natural reasoning in even the best of philosophers cannot without humility and submission arrive at the knowledge of the Christian God (iv.6–7). The general optimism of the earlier dialogues is replaced by a general recognition of the effect of human fallenness.

This deeper recognition of human fallenness occasions Augustine's development of the theory of personal evil in terms of carnal *consuetudo*. He draws on the Manichees for insights of experience of personal evil, borrowing from them the double notion of "wickedness" and "mortality," although he has substantially transformed these simplistic ideas into an elaborate theory that eventually does away with dualism. In his notion of *consuetudo*, therefore, Augustine means to tackle the problem of the inability of humans to escape from the trap of corruption. Certainly, divine aid will be necessary for one to get out of the trap; nevertheless, whether one is free to turn to God for help remains open. This last issue is addressed in the following affirmation:

> If, however, while living in this course of human life, the soul overcomes those desires which it fed on for its own destruction by enjoying mortal things, and believes that it is helped by God's grace to overcome them, serving God with the mind and a good will, it will undoubtedly be restored, and will turn again from the many mutable things to the immutable One [...].[28]

Restoration is granted because of human good will (also xxxv.65). Remaining firm in his anti-Manichaean position, Augustine insists that the human will that operates freely can choose whether to rely on divine help and guidance in ordering one's life. Grace plays only a supplementary role, to enable the realization of what the good will has decided,[29] that will which also conditions the affections, or the movements of the soul (xiv.28).

To understand Augustine's analysis of the extent of the influence of the fall on humans, we must grasp his "tripartite" anthropology of rational soul, irrational soul and the body. He has assumed, it seems, that the fall has left the rational soul untouched as far as the exercise of free will is concerned, although the other two are affected (xxiii.44). An analysis of the will (*uoluntas*) in *Contra Fortunatum* (392) as well as in Augustine's later exposition in *fid. sym.* x.23 (393) confirms this.[30] In the latter reference, he explicitly states his "tripartite" anthropology and correlates the spirit, soul and body with his previous notion of rational soul, irrational soul and body.[31] He differentiates between the spirit and the soul in their readiness for submission:

> But the soul is not as easily subjected to the spirit for doing good work, as is the spirit to God for acquiring true faith and good will. Yet sometimes, with difficulty, its impulse which melts away in carnal and temporal things is restrained. But [...] even it is cleansed, receiving the stability of its nature under the rule of the spirit.[32]

By its very nature, the soul is submissive to the spirit, just as the spirit submits to God. But when the soul turns instead to carnal things, it is "called flesh" (*caro nominatur*) and resists the spirit.[33] Augustine thus addresses the issue of the effect of the mortal body as visible flesh on the carnal affection of the soul, but he has nothing to say about the effect on the spirit.

It is recognized that in *Contra Fortunatum* (392) Augustine, due to Fortunatus' invocation of Pauline support for the notion of the inevitability of evil, is forced to focus on Paul's notion of the flesh as an intrinsic principle rebellious to what is instituted by God. Prior to the debate with Fortunatus, Augustine has already cited Rom. 7:25 to support his idea of *consuetudo facta cum carne* in *mus.* VI.xi.33. Yet Fortunatus' appeal to the same group of biblical verses of Rom. 8:7 and 7:23–25 certainly leaves Augustine with no option but to study Paul's writings more seriously (*Fort.* 21). Even here, we have not yet noted any significant change of position from that in *De uera religione*. In this later work, formation of bad habits is described as "carnal knowledge" (*carnis prudentia*) that makes a person unable to submit to God's law, until he or she is liberated when God's grace breathes divine love into the soul (*Fort.* 22). In spite of the emphasis on the "necessity" of personal evil, the issue is only about human inability to will to do good. It is not yet concerned with whether one is unable to turn to God for help.

In the first phase of the transition, Augustine's focus is on the human inability to live rightly unless divinely aided. But help is always available and restoration made possible to all of good will. Salvation is potentially universal in so far as there is human willingness. Human will is considered free at the rational level to choose to turn to God for help despite moral difficulties. As regards the maintenance of the cosmic order, Augustine shows no observable change from his previous assertion, and this remains the case as long as the human will is deemed to have the final arbitration whether to turn to God (with or without the help of grace to complete the conversion process). Sinning is always possible for created rational beings because they are from nothing, yet God can keep his creation from being vitiated, and even restore what is vitiated to wholeness. Meantime, by punishing evil, God preserves the beauty of the whole creation (*uer. rel.* xix.37, xxiii.44).

Second phase (393–394). Augustine continues to bring out the ramifications of the idea of *consuetudo* at the beginning of phase two. In *De sermone domini in monte* I, composed between 393 and 394, one can however perceive a shift of attention toward *concupiscentia*. This work is for the instruction of Christian perfection (*ser. dom.* I.i.1). In discussing how sin occurs, Augustine distinguishes three stages: suggestion, pleasure, and consent (*suggestione delectatione consensione*). While suggestion or persuasion comes from temptation, and a feeling of pleasure results in habit formation, it is the human will that ultimately determines whether there is consent.[34] Habit is formed by repeated sinning as greater pleasure is derived each time. Habit plays a role in making consent to sin much more appealing. Thus, if one sins before the habit is formed, one sins more greatly (xii.34). Augustine explicitly suggests here that *consuetudo* is the means by which carnal pleasure (cf. *concupiscentia*) can operate in us to take us captive; the process can be reversed only by imploring Christ's help (xii.36).

Thus, to lead an orderly moral life, one needs to exercise the good will so that the irrationality of the soul may be subdued and the soul become subject to God (ii.9). This point is carefully elaborated in his commentary on the beatitudes. Through humility, one would be informed by Scripture to attain true knowledge and be assisted by divine aid to fight off the entanglement of carnal *consuetudo* and sins. Augustine puts special emphasis on humility (*humilitas*) as the perpetual starting-point of the process (iii.10; also iv.11; xi.32; xxii.74),[35] thus making it the means of engendering good will. With this qualification, Augustine clarifies that his notion of good will is not so much a mental exertion as a yielding to God.[36]

Along with the assertion of humility as the starting-point to conversion, the idea of foreknowledge in relation to divine judgment is first mentioned here. A hint of election may also be detected. These elements are conducive to Augustine's construction of his theory of election by divine foreknowledge of the human good will. Foreknowledge is mentioned in the context of the prediction of divine judgment. God's judgment could be foretold by a prophet or Christ himself because they foresaw human "unbelief" or "works" of wickedness (xxi.72). Those who have once been in the Christian fellowship and later rejected it cannot be saved again and there is no use praying for their salvation, because they "have chosen to be incurable" (*insanabiles esse uoluerunt*) (xxii.77). Their condemnation is also foreknown and thus can also be foretold (xxii.76). At this point, Augustine considers salvation as guaranteed only to those who persevere to the end. To him, to become a child of God is a process gradually realized as we obey God's commandments by divine aid. In his words: "we are made sons by the power received, inasfar as we implement those things commanded by Him. [...] Therefore He does not say, Do those things, since you are sons; but, Do those things, that you may be sons."[37] It is true that God has called us to the eternal inheritance through his Son by granting us sonship. But whether the "wisdom" (*sapientia*) leading to salvation and the "teaching of truth" (*doctrina ueritatis*) are available to everyone indiscriminately is doubtful. Augustine is undecided whether God's goodness causes the "Sun of righteousness," i.e., Christ, to shine upon both good and evil men, or whether his goodness only restricts the spiritual Sun from rising except on the good and holy. Despite his indecision, Augustine prefers the latter option, which has a flavor of election (xxiii.79).

It is not hard to see that once Augustine is convinced of the reality of election, the pieces of his theory of divine election by foreknowledge will readily fall into place. If God does elect only a limited number of people for salvation, he would choose those whom he foresees as good and holy. But, admitting that good deeds are ultimately initiated by good will, Augustine can logically conclude that God chooses according to his foreknowledge of the good will in his elect.

As Augustine focuses more on the Pauline writings, the shift of attention from *consuetudo* to *concupiscentia* hinted at in Book One of *De sermone domine in monte* becomes more apparent in *Expositio quarumdam propositionum ex Epistula ad Romanos* (394), his first systematic commentary on the Book of Romans. This shift from philosophical to theological attention concurs with his change of framework for the portrayal of salvation history. Previously in the mode of philosophical ascent, the frame is the six day creation (*Gen. Man.* I.xxiii.35–xxiv.42). But now, to reflect the theological concern of the human inner struggle, Augustine introduces the four stages of human life in relation to God's law and its fulfillment.[38] These are the stages: prior to the Law, under the Law, under grace, and in peace. In the first, we assent to sin; in the second, we do not want to sin but still are overcome by it; in the third, we triumph over sin by divine help; in the fourth, we are transformed in resurrection. Augustine remarks that, unlike the first man who was free not to sin, all of us after him can only choose to not want to sin. The only fruitful exercise of this freedom of choice is to seek divine help, for the more one wants to attain righteousness by fulfilling the requirement of the Law with self-effort, the more one's concupiscence is roused (*exp. Rom.* 37:44, 29:37). Without forsaking the theory of *consuetudo*, Augustine sees the Pauline notion of *concupiscentia* as a more intrinsic problematic in regard to the effect of human fallenness. Babcock notes Augustine's heightened awareness of human fallenness in his understanding of Rom. 7:25a: "For the first time, then, Augustine has pictured a human state in which a person must struggle against a self which is not merely resistant to the will, but is actually beyond his own control, which conquers him rather than being conquered by him."[39] Hence, Augustine remarks:

> [Paul] calls the law of sin the mortal condition due to the transgression of Adam, under which condition we are made mortal. For due to this fall of the flesh, carnal concupiscence rouses us.[40]

Those who give in to concupiscence will be captured by it (39:47). Therefore, not only does the fall render us vulnerable to the formation of evil *consuetudo*; it has also made us intrinsically rebellious to the appeal of moral order from the Law. The notion of *concupiscentia* portrays a far more serious effect of human fallenness than did the notion of *consuetudo*.

In addition to dealing with a more profound human inability to overcome sin without divine aid, Augustine has to come to terms with the biblical teaching on election. Quoting Mt. 22:14, he is convinced of the fact that only a few of those called are chosen. And Rom. 8:28 supplies the reason: only those who are "called according to [his] purpose" (*secundum propositum uocati*) are justified. As for explaining the mechanism behind election, Augustine takes his cue from the subsequent verse which says: "Since those whom he foreknew he also predestined to be conformed to the image of his son."[41] As he succinctly puts it:

> For not all who are called are called according to a purpose, for this purpose pertains to the foreknowledge and predestination of God. Nor has God predestined anyone except the one whom God has foreknown would believe and would follow the call. Such persons, he [Paul] calls "the elect." For many do not come, though they have been called; but no one comes who has not been called.[42]

Illustrating with the election of Jacob over Esau, Augustine states that it is faith, not deeds, that is the point of merit which God foreknows (52:60). In his thinking, some kind of *meritum* as a criterion for election is necessary if election is not to become arbitrary, "for all are equal prior to merit, and election cannot be made in the case of entirely equal things."[43] Thus, even though good deeds are considered God's work, belief is accounted ours. (This close association between "merit" and "free will" later leads Augustine to reject his early view of election, because there is no logical distinction between divine foreknowledge of free will or of work if they are both counted as merit.) There is a dynamic interplay between God's grace and human merit:

> But grace is such that the call is proposed beforehand to the sinner when he has merited nothing other than damnation. For if the called has followed the caller—something done indeed out of free choice—he will merit even the Holy Spirit, through whom good works can be performed, and by remaining in the Spirit—which is nonetheless by free choice—he will also merit eternal life, which cannot be corrupted by any blemish.[44]

The starting point is grace by way of divine calling. The human response by the exercise of the will determines the efficacy of the calling on each individual, with respect to both conversion and perseverance.[45] There can be no willing prior to the call, and there is no divine help without the willing as response. As illustrated in the hardening of Pharaoh's heart, the withholding of divine aid is a just judgment on account of Pharaoh's lack of faith engendered from good will (54:62). God's grace, therefore, makes salvation available to all but his justice limits it only to the deserving.

Although Pharaoh's case may be used to support Augustine's assertion of the centrality of faith, it does not necessitate divine foreknowledge as the explanation for election. In fact, Augustine says that Pharaoh had "merited" his hardness of heart by his *prior infidelitas* (54:62) or *occulta superioris impietas* (hidden preceding impiety) (55:63). The idea of hiddenness which will be developed further in the next phase of the transition is already emerging.[46] This idea seems to refer to the specific incidents of preceding impiety by which God judges in secret, but not to the reason for divine rejection which is the "preceding impiety" itself.

In the second phase of the transition, Augustine has deepened his understanding of the seriousness of the effect of the fall. Even though he has further developed the concept of *consuetudo* in *De sermone domini in monte* I, he finds that the Pauline notion of *concupiscentia* as an intrinsic rebellious force against moral order addresses the heart of the problem of fallenness. Regarding the possibility of restoration, he has to face a new issue of limited salvation. While still maintaining that some kind of human merit should be the basis for God's electing, Augustine proposes the solution of election by divine foreknowledge of human good will. Although this idea of election has not contradicted his earlier view, it definitely points toward the assertion that the outcome of an individual's eternal salvation is to be incorporated into God's cosmic ordering. This tendency will become clearer in the third phase, but is already hinted at here by the introduction of the notion of "hiddenness."

Third phase (395–396). The significance of this last transitional phase (and later) is no longer the explicit identification of the influence of *concupiscentia* but its logical ramification in the development of the idea of election. Hence, hereafter we will not seek for any new emphasis or understanding Augustine might have concerning that notion, but we must follow through the change initiated by his attention to the notion as the intrinsic rebellious principle against God's law. For this reason, we will make constant comparisons between the current and the former ideas.

As the first work in this last phase, the second book of *De sermone domini in monte* is not merely a continuation of the exposition interrupted at the end of Book One. There is sufficient evidence to show that it was composed around the middle of 395,[47] quite some time after the first book had been completed. From consideration of the content alone, the second book has a different, though related, concern with respect to Book One. While one of the central themes of the first book is the necessity of humility for human good will to start the conversion process toward God and of help in being restored to an orderly life, the second book is concerned with purity and simplicity of the heart to maintain undivided focus on God for the conduct of one's life (e.g., *ser. dom.* II.i.1), in view of attaining the wisdom of salvation (xxv.86). Though the necessity of the "simplicity of the heart" (*simplicitas cordis*) is mentioned elsewhere in the context of perceiving spiritual truth (*uer. rel.* xxxv.65), *De sermone domini in monte* II is the first major exposition of this theme in relation to conduct. Hence, at this point of development, we may say that simplicity of heart is able to overcome the dual problem of fallen humanity: ignorance in regard to the perception of truth, and difficulty in conducting oneself rightly.

Despite this new focus on simplicity, the previous idea of good will as a proper and free response to the divine call is still very much alive, as illustrated in Augustine's explanation of "on earth peace to men of good will" (Lk. 2:14): "[...] when our good will has gone before, following the one who calls, may the will of God be perfected in us".[48] The grace of God is his call to be God's children, grace that precedes our asking (iv.16). But our starting-point is still a humble response to this grace (xxiii.77; cf. xi.38). In regard to the attainment of truth, we are exhorted to ask, seek and knock (xxi.71). As the human will turns to God, the body, though prone to the weakness of carnal habit, will obey the spirit or soul (vi.23). It is in this conversion to God that one's inner heart is purged to become pure and simple (iii.14).

In this work, Augustine tends to shy away from mentioning foreknowledge. If election by foreknowledge is anticipated in Book One, and prominent in the early part of *Expositio quarumdam propositionum ex Epistula ad Romanos*, the same is not true here. Divine foreknowledge receives only a casual mention, in a context perfectly suited to an elaboration on the theme of election. The sixth petition of the Lord's prayer on temptation may not, at first sight, be thought to have anything to do with election. But Augustine obviously treats the withholding of divine assistance as a related issue. Concerning this, he has chosen to speak of "the most hidden order and merit" (*ordo occultissimus ac merita*) as the explanation (ix.30). Moreover, in regard to the relation between the notion of temptation and election, it is interesting to observe how Augustine uses his comment on Dt. 13:3, which explains that God tests us not because he does not know us, for he is omniscient, but because he wants us to know ourselves. While Augustine uses this comment as a prelude to his exposition of the theory of election by foreknowledge in *exp. Rom.* 46:54–47:55, he employs the same exposition disjointly with the theme of hidden divine judgment in *ser. dom.* II.ix.30–32.

Although the association of merit with divine ordering is not new (e.g., *uer. rel.* xxiii.44), the stress on the hiddenness of ordering and its use as an explanation for withdrawal of divine aid are.[49] Immediately after this affirmation of secrecy in divine ordering, Augustine follows up by asserting that the reason for withholding divine help is *often known* (*ser.*

dom. II.ix.30). This implies hiddenness in *some* cases of which the true reason cannot be known. Here, he seems to be struggling toward a fully predestinarian view. We try to reconstruct his reasoning by following the ensuing argument. In reference to *exp. Rom.* 47:55–54:62, it is not difficult to conjecture that the reason for God's judgment of Pharaoh is known: lack of faith. This then begs the question of which cases of divine judgment could be unknown. If Augustine is forsaking his theory of election by foreknowledge, then what is *unknown* to Augustine at this moment would appear to be the election of Jacob over Esau before they were born. This is the much quoted supportive illustration for his mature view of election since *Simpl.* I.ii.16. That what bothers Augustine now is indeed the election of Jacob might be confirmed in his later reference to the hiddenness of divine ordering in the context of a full-blown notion of predestination (*Faus.* XXII.78). There, possibly alluding to Jacob's case, he admits that the reason one person receives mercy and another does not is unknown.[50] With this later view, not just *some* but *all* cases of divine judgment lie hidden. Hence, we may conclude that Augustine's emphasis on the hiddenness of divine ordering at this point signals a gradual shift toward a more predestinarian view. The idea of hiddenness of divine judgment reflects his attempt to incorporate the notion of election into the secret divine operation of the cosmic order.

That Augustine is giving up his theory of election by divine foreknowledge is also reflected in his explanation of selective calling. In his comment on Jesus' teaching about not giving what is holy to dogs and pearls to swine, Augustine believes that Jesus practiced his own teaching by directing his salvific message only to those who were able to receive it, even in the presence of others. In other words, the message was issued in a certain way, so that only the intended audience might respond to it. This idea is akin to his mature view except that, for now, the determining factor in the response is still the inner disposition or readiness of the hearers at the time of receiving the message (*ser. dom.* II.xx.70). As such, divine foreknowledge is unnecessary in the process of election.

In Book Two, the conditions for a mature view of grace are ripening and the seminal concepts are already at hand: the previous view of election by foreknowledge is dropped, the more predestinarian notion of hidden divine judgment is mentioned, and the mode of selective calling is worked out. Nevertheless, the part on human initiative in the restoration process is still significant: to humble oneself and to keep one's heart simple. Augustine might be thinking that, at least in most cases, God's knowledge of the readiness of one's inner disposition (instead of *fore*knowledge of faith) is the condition for election. But as soon as Augustine is convinced of the total inability of the human initiative and the total hiddenness of divine judgment, the formulation of his mature view is just a matter of time. These two conditions are only logical conclusions of Augustine's understanding of *concupiscentia* as the intrinsic evil principle of rebellion under the condition of limited salvation. If it is truly intrinsic, it would no doubt affect the whole operation of the human will. And owing to the will's inability to take the initiative in converting to God, there is no explicitly comprehensible ground for specific individual elections. Therefore, we might reason from the logical point of view that, given the framework of cosmic order, the only other factor needed besides the notion of *concupiscentia* for Augustine to arrive at his mature view of grace is the notion of limited salvation, which is inspired by the biblical idea of election.[51]

Question 68 of *De diuersis quaestionibus 83*, written between 395 and 396, is the last point in the transition. It was probably composed after *De sermone domini in monte* II but before *Ad Simplicianum*.[52] Though the ground covered by this question is like that in *exp. Rom.* 52:60–54:62, there are subtle differences in the two treatments.[53] First, the text is again silent about the role of divine foreknowledge in divine election or judgment. The focus is primarily on the one obvious case of divine judgment—Pharaoh's hardness of heart as a just desert due to his prior infidelity as shown in his mistreatment of Israel (*diu. quaes.*, quest. 68, 4). Only at the end is the election of Jacob over Esau hastily dealt with. Augustine does not really try to explain how it happened, except to ascribe it to the lofty and profound decree of God which only perhaps the most saintly person with perfect love for God will be able to comprehend (6). In order to accuse the materialistic Manichees of spiritual blindness, Augustine at the beginning is forced to affirm that God's judgment is knowable to the spiritual, as he has previously asserted (1; cf. *exp. Rom.* 54:62); he seems unable to maintain this view at the end. This situation agrees with what we have suspected already in our treatment of *De sermone domini in monte* II: divine judgment is deemed more and more hidden as Augustine progresses toward the mature view.

Although Augustine still wants to assert that God prejudges a person according to the "most hidden merit" (*occultissima merita*) of faith (*diu. quaes.*, quest. 68, 3 & 4),[54] it is not clear whether he would maintain that good will is entirely the result of one's deliberation. Good will is certainly needed to respond to God's call prior to the coming of God's mercy, but the good willing itself can be due to God's special working in his calling:

"And since no one can will unless admonished and called, whether inside where no man sees, or outside through the sound of speech or through some other visible signs, it happens that God may *work* in us even our very act of willing" (my emphasis).[55] Augustine uses the subjunctive form of *operor* (i.e., to work), which may reflect his unwillingness at this point to fully ascribe the forming of the human will to God's action. The above is not yet a clear statement on prevenient grace, but is Augustine's attempt to grapple with Rom. 9:16: "it is not of him who wills nor of him who runs, but of God who shows mercy,"[56] a verse he did not treat in *Expositio quarumdam propositionum ex Epistula ad Romanos*. As never before, rather than merely dealing with the sequence of calling-willing-mercy, Augustine here is exploring how human willing may be attributed to God's work. His answer seems to indicate his preference to God's increasing participation in one's willing well. If this is so, the idea of God's working in one's willing is one step closer to Augustine's mature view, beyond the notion of selective calling (rendered successful in those who are readily disposed to have good will), noted in our treatment of *De sermone domini in monte* II.

The final transition to the mature view is marked by the phasing out of the idea of election by foreknowledge. The interim view of election by divine knowledge of one's inner disposition stays only for a short time. As Augustine diminishes the place of human initiative, increasingly he ascribes election to the hiddenness of divine judgment. Although human good will is still needed to respond to God's call for salvation, God seems to be playing an ever more significant role in inducing such a response.

Mature Stage (396–400)

It is well recognized by scholars that the ideas in *Ad Simplicianum* I, written in 396, represent Augustine's first mature view on grace.[57] We find that this maturation is not without a prelude of gradual development until the elimination of human will as an independent factor in the causal chain of personal salvation. In many ways, Augustine's ideas in his response to Simplicianus' first question in 396 are reminiscent of those in his preceding writings.[58] Humility is the prerequisite for divine aid (*Simpl.* I.i.5). Humans are held captive to sin because of *concupiscentia*, the byproduct of inherited mortality, and of *consuetudo*. While *consuetudo* unceasingly binds a person to sin during his or her worldly life, mortality as an inherited nature is the penalty for the guilt of "original sin" (*peccatum originale*) (i.10–11).[59] We are free to will but unable to act rightly according to the will (i.11–12) unless we turn to God for help (i.14).

In the second question, Augustine for the first time explicitly argues against his former position that God elects by foreknowing one's faith. (This position, according to our observation, was quietly dropped when he wrote *De sermone domini in monte* II.) His point is that there is no logical difference between foreknowing faith and foreknowing works, for both imply humans as initiators of the election process (ii.5–6; cf. *exp. Rom.* 55:63). Augustine considers his former view of election by merit as one judged according to equity (*Simpl.* I.ii.4). Now, he tries to build up his case on grace by first recalling his point in question 68 of *De diuersis quaestionibus 83* that God's grace first appears in his call, either by a hidden admonition in one's mind or outwardly through the bodily senses. From this calling comes an incipient faith which Augustine likens to conception (ii.2). Even though the sequence of calling-faith-good works is clear, the proportion of input between God and humankind in the right application of faith still needs exploration. Augustine tries to preserve both. It is by God's grace that the call is issued and that we are able to do right, but Augustine also affirms that the responsibility to follow God's call is ours:

> In one way God presents us with the ability to will and in another way he presents us the thing to be willed. As regards the ability to will, he wills it to be his and ours, his in terms of calling, ours in terms of following. But what we may actually will he alone gives, and that is, to be able to act well and to live happily always.[60]

Since not all who are called are chosen, the question is whether we can use our will to resist God's grace in calling. Augustine's response is that only those chosen will respond favorably because God knows how to call them in such a way that they will respond "in conformity" (*congruenter*): this is the effectual cause of human good will (ii.13–14). Though God is not said to impose his will on the elect, he indeed works in such a way as to stimulate the human will to respond. In considering this, Augustine certainly takes seriously human psychological dynamics, as in the role of human willing in prayer (ii.21).[61] In his words: "The will itself can in no way be moved unless something suggests itself that would delight and induce the soul."[62] Thus, considered psychologically, the human will is free, but the outcome of the willing is divinely arranged and therefore guaranteed.

Nevertheless, if God knows how to effectually call each person, then why are some left not chosen, as in the case of Esau? Augustine reiterates that God is just in withholding mercy since all sinners are justly condemned. But for a solution as to why one is chosen and another not,

Augustine has to appeal to God's secret arrangement (ii.16), to an election whose reasoning is hidden from us, but is nevertheless in congruence with God's cosmic ordering. Augustine exhorts his reader:

> Only let us believe, even if we are unable to grasp it, that he who made and laid the foundation for the whole creation, spiritual and corporeal, arranges all things by number, weight and measure. But his judgments are inscrutable and his ways past finding out.[63]

There is good that ensues even from God's punishment of sinners, which serves as an object lesson to the elect (ii.20).

An important development in *Contra Faustum* (397–398/399) is the explicit link between the concept of cosmic order which is hidden from us and that of predestination which is God's secret arrangement. This linkage was only hinted at in the closing sentences of *Ad Simplicianum* I (ii.22) just cited. From Augustine's perspective, God's administering of his hidden arrangement to confer grace and pass judgment is an ordering of good and evil (*Faus.* XXI.2–3). It then seems logical for him to make God's secret administration of salvation part of the grand cosmic order, as he himself puts it in this citation:

> But the causes for the *distribution of judgment and mercy of God*, why one this and another that, are hidden, though just. All the same, however, we are not ignorant that all these things are done by reason of either the judgment or mercy of God; although in concealment, by means of measures and numbers and weights all is arranged by God, the Creator of *all that exists in nature* (my emphasis).[64]

Compared with the early concept of the two-tiered structure, we notice here a change in the framework. Before, what constitutes the cosmic order is God's *judgment* of the moral universe and his ordering of creation. Now, it is God's *election and judgment* being subsumed under the frame of cosmic order. While the outcome of the individual salvation in the former case is not predetermined, the latter case reflects the determinism that is inherent in the notion of effectual calling.

This change is also carried through in the distinction between holy angels and humankind. Earlier, in *lib. arb.* III.v.15 (395), Augustine believed this to be a matter of difference in the *exercise of free will*. The holy angels will to turn to God always, whereas man can will either way. God's omnipotent governance is shown in his foreknowledge and judgment in both situations. First, God foresees human willing and makes a judgment on every person (iii.6) by placing each at his or her suitable place in the cosmic order (v.12) to preserve the beauty of the universe (ix.26–27). Second, God foreknows the willing of angels and assigns them their proper function (xi.33). But here in *Contra Faustum*, Augustine thinks that angels are different from humankind by having a *superior nature* which will also be realized in the righteous but only in the *eschaton*.[65] By drawing a line between the temporal nature of human beings and the superior nature of the elect in eternity, Augustine is doing nothing less than affirming that God's governance in matters of personal salvation is based on his eternal law that sets the universal order of things (*Faus.* XXII.27, 28). These points are reiterated in the last book of *Confessiones* within the context of cosmic order.

The doctrine of grace expressed in *Ad Simplicianum* works through, in *Confessiones* XIII (400), all the elements regarding predestination and election. It is prevenient grace that prepares the soul before one responds to God's calling (i.1). Not by human merit, but by grace, some are set apart from the rest of the sinful mass (xiv.15; xvii.20). Augustine explicitly asserts that these are the ones whom God has already secretly called at the beginning of the world, before the firmament was made (xxiii.33). Also, he affirms that predestination was before all times but is to be accomplished in time (xxxiv.49). Such acknowledgment admits that each one's destiny is fixed in the eternal plan of God, which could well be a part of the cosmic ordering. Obviously, this is Augustine's understanding of his own salvation (*conf.* V.ix.17).[66]

To support this interpretation, we refer to Augustine's comment that not only is the overall harmonious order of the creation very good (xxviii.43), but even more so is the parallel relation between predestination and creation (xxxiv.49), thus implying that the two belong to the same grand order. Immediately after summarizing the account of creation, he says:

> We have also examined, according to the figurative understanding, those things you willed either to be made in such an order or to be written in such an order. We see, because each thing is good, and all are very good, in your Word, in your Only-begotten, heaven and earth, the head and the body of the Church, in predestination before all times, without morning and evening.[67]

Augustine alludes to his earlier passage where he asserts that God has made in his Christ "heaven and earth," the spiritual and carnal parts of his Church (xii.13). The parallelism between creation and predestination in these two parts of the Church is realized in the spiritual creation of holy angels and in the spiritual re-creation of redeemed humankind. Both have taken place in Christ and by the work of the Spirit being borne over the unruly water (viii.9; xii.13). If both angels and redeemed humans are rational creatures, then they could be equally important in the cosmic hierarchy and are not necessarily different in the *eschaton*. Again, if the creation of holy angels is part of God's eternal plan, then it is logical to think that the redeemed humans are also elected according to the same plan.

Here, in the final development of Augustine's initial mature view of grace, we observe unmistakably the total subsumption of the moral or rational order, including angels and humans alike, under the grand cosmic ordering. As such, the determinism inspired by the Manichaean notion of the Good in terms of the concepts of *consuetudo* and *concupiscentia*, under the aspect of limited salvation, is brought to its logical conclusion. In total, we have shown a threefold influence of the Manichaean notion of the Good in Augustine's development of the doctrine of predestination: the context of Supreme Good, the framework in cosmic order, and the deterministic factor exercised by *consuetudo* and *concupiscentia*.

CONCLUSION

We set out to determine how Augustine's understanding of the Manichaean idea of the Good affects his own idea of the Good and of related notions, in particular, Supreme Good, personal evil, and predestination. We have shown that he perceives this Manichaean idea to be equated with the Beautiful, understood as that which engenders tranquil pleasure. To achieve tranquility through contemplation of the Supreme Good was the goal he set in his earliest writing, *De pulchro et apto*. This perspective continued to be at work in his insistence that God, as the Supreme Good, is the guarantor of the soul's tranquil enjoyment.

To tackle the issue of personal evil, Augustine borrowed from the Manichees their dual notion of evil as "wickedness" and as "mortality." These were considered evil because they are the antithesis of tranquil pleasure at the spiritual and the physical levels of existence. He shared with the Manichees the view that these aspects of evil are inevitable so long as life is lived in this world. Together, these borrowed approaches to evil helped Augustine to formulate an alternative explanation of the principle of personal evil, encapsulated in his notions of *consuetudo* and *concupiscentia*.

The Manichaean contribution to Augustine's ideas of Supreme Good and personal evil, therefore, lies in the concept of tranquil pleasure, the subjective criterion in the appropriation of the Good. On the other hand, the Manichaean influence on the doctrine of predestination is limited to structural matters, with two *caveats*. First, the framework of cosmic order within which Augustine developed his doctrine is a result of his response to the Manichaean view of the universe as a mixture of good and evil. In this response, he again employs the Manichaean idea of the Good to affirm that the whole universe is beautiful despite the presence of evil. So long as evil is put in its proper place, the cosmic harmony is preserved. Second, this framework undergoes structural change as Augustine took more seriously the inevitability of personal evil. In the end, the ordering of both the physical and the spiritual creation—including the election of individuals for salvation—is assigned to the province of the divine eternal law.

Why does the development of the doctrine of predestination have to wait until the time of Augustine's anti-Manichaean polemics? What did the Manichees bring to the debate on the problem of evil to facilitate the process? Are Augustine's polemics against the Manichees truly indispensable for his conception of predestination? As mentioned by J. Pelikan, the theological climate in Augustine's time fostered free will and responsibility. Determinism would have gone against the tide.[1] This observation may be illustrated by Ambrose's understanding of the lives of Jacob and Esau, a favorite example for Augustine in explaining his notion of predestination. Of the few references in Ambrose's corpus that mention the two brothers, only one treats the radically different outcome between their lives at a theoretical level. According to Ambrose, Jacob and Esau represent from the same initial condition of one womb two human natures of good and evil, not two human destinies of salvation and damnation.[2] This moral interpretation suggests that Ambrose lacks sensitivity to the cosmological implications of the case. Not only does Ambrose in general show little interest in determinism, he does not seem to be motivated to dwell for long on the idea of the irresistibility of evil, even though he makes ample reference to evil *consuetudo* and *concupiscentia*, sometimes mentioned together with "flesh" (*caro*), "passion" (*libido*) and "lust" (*cupiditas*).[3] So, for Ambrose, who mirrors the theological climate of Augustine's time, a strong commitment to the idea of the inevitability of personal evil and to the notion of determinism—the two basic building blocks of a predestinarian theory—is lacking. It would be interesting to pursue further the whole question of the Christian discussion of *consuetudo*, *concupiscentia* and predeterminism prior to Augustine.

A significant Manichaean contribution to the debate on the problem of evil is the question, Whence comes evil? (*unde sit malum?*) (*mor.* II.ii.2), which addresses the above concerns. The interrogative term "whence" (*unde*) not only asks about the cause or etiology of personal evil, but, viewed in light of the cosmological context of the Manichaean myth, also pursues the question of the destiny of the human soul. The Manichaean explanation for the cause of personal evil is relatively straightforward. One cannot escape from moral evil because there is a metaphysical evil principle at work behind the soul. In other words, one sins involuntarily.[4] Considered cosmologically, the human soul is thrown into the predicament of constant struggle with evil not by its own choice but by the determination of an external factor. According to the

Manichaean myth, this factor is the good principle or the God who sends the good soul to be mixed with evil in order to block the invasion of an advancing enemy (*mor.* II.xii.25; *Faus.* XX.17, XXII.22; *Fort.* 7; *nat. bon.* xlii).

The Manichaean question of "Whence comes evil?" had captured the attention of the young Augustine (*lib. arb.* I.ii.4), perhaps due to his personal difficulties in resisting sin (cf. *conf.* II.i.1). His interest in the question did not diminish after his conversion. His first attempt as a Christian to look for the root of evil is registered in *lib. arb.* I.iii.8–iv.10. Here, he tried to develop a theory that would do away with determinism. His approach was to confine the ultimate cause of evil to the irrationality of the self so that God might not be implicated in the predetermination of one's destiny (as is the case in Manichaean teaching). The theory of personal evil finds its mature expression in Augustine's conceptions of *consuetudo* and *concupiscentia* (around 390). Nonetheless, once he began responding to the Manichaean view regarding the macrocosm, he could not avoid the issue of determinism. In his alternative proposal, divine cosmic ordering, Augustine had to address the question of what ultimately determines an individual's place in the universal order. Since the more deeply one is bonded to evil, the less one is able to control one's destiny, the belief in the inevitability of personal evil would then imply a view that the determination is made by the God who orders the cosmos.[5] Expressed in the language of predestination, this view means that God has the power to elect from the *massa damnata* those who receive salvation and to leave the rest in damnation.[6]

Augustine's response to the Manichaean question of "Whence comes evil?" is indispensable to his development of the doctrine of predestination. Although other Christian leaders, Ambrose included, had responded to the challenge of Manichaeism, it appears that only Augustine seriously engaged this specific Manichaean question, not by way of mere reaction, but by intelligently deploying Manichaean categories—always with new contents—to address the Manichaean issues of determinism and evil.

NOTES

Introduction

1 J. Rist, "Plotinus and Augustine on Evil," in *Plotino e il Neoplatonismo in Oriente e in Occidente*, Convegno internazionale, Roma, 5–9 ottobre 1970, (Problemi attuali di scienza e di cultura, 198) (Roma: Accademia Nazionale dei Lincei, 1974), 495–508; S. MacDonald, "Augustine's Christian-Platonist Account of Goodness," *The New Scholasticism* 63 (1989): 485–509.

2 S. Kikushi, "On Augustine's Understanding of the Created Good," *Studies in Medieval Thought* 31 (1989): 76–83; D.H. Nikkel, "St. Augustine on the Goodness of Creaturely Existence," *The Duke Divinity School Review* 43 (1978): 181–187.

3 *Augustine on Human Goodness: Metaphysics, Ethics and Politics*, Proceedings of the 21st Annual Philosophy Colloquium, Dayton, Apr. 7–9, 1994, dir. R. Herbenick & P.A. Johnson, published in *University of Dayton Review* 22 (1994).

4 P. Slater, "Goodness as Order and Harmony in Augustine," in *Augustine: From Rhetor to Theologian*, eds. J. McWilliam, et al. (Waterloo, ON: Wilfrid Laurier University Press, 1992), 151–159; R.M. Cooper, "Saint Augustine's Doctrine of Evil," *Scottish Journal of Theology* 16 (1963): 256–276.

5 E.g., F. Berthold, "Free Will and Theodicy in Augustine: An Exposition and Critique," *Religious Studies* 17 (1981): 525–535; G.H. Ranson, "Augustine's Account of the Nature and Origin of Moral Evil," *Review and Expositor: A Baptist Theological Journal* 50 (1953): 309–322.

6 J.M. Salas Martínez, "La maravillosa y misteriosa bondad de Dios hacia el hombre según San Augustín especialmente en sus escritos contra el Pelagianismo y Semipelagianismo" (Diss., Fac. Theol. Pontificiae Universitatis Gregorianae, Romae, 1964).

7 While N. Fischer's article in *Augustinus-Lexikon* gives a comprehensive survey on Augustine's notion of the Good, it is no more than a passing note when it comes to addressing the question of Manichaean influence. See C. Mayer, et al., eds. *Augustinus-Lexikon* (Basel: Schwabe, 1986–1994), s.v. "Bonum," by N. Fischer.

8 Worthy of mention is G. Wenning, "Der Einfluß des Manichäismus und des Ambrosius auf die Hermeneutik Augustins," *Revue des études augustiniennes* 36 (1990): 80–90.

9   J. Van Oort, "Augustin und der Manichäismus," *Zeitschrift für Religions- und Geistesgeschichte* 46 (1994): 126–127. Also, *idem*, "Augustine and Mani on Concupiscentia Sexualis," in *Augustiniana Traiectina,* communications présentées au colloque international d'Utrecht, 13–14 novembre 1986, eds. J. Den Boeft & J. Van Oort (Paris: Études augustiniennes, 1987), 137; *idem*, "Augustine on Sexual Concupiscence and Original Sin," in *Studia Patristica* 22, papers presented to the Tenth International Conference on Patristic Studies held in Oxford 1987, ed. E.A. Livingstone (Leuven: Peeters Press, 1989), 385; J.K. Coyle, *Augustine's "De Moribus Ecclesiae Catholicae": A Study of the Work, its Composition and its Sources* (Paradosis, 25) (Fribourg: University Press, 1978), 6; G. Bonner, *St. Augustine of Hippo: Life and Controversies*, revised ed. (Norwich: The Canterbury Press, 1986), 194; M.A. Vannier, "Manichéisme et pensée augustinienne de la création," in *Collectanea Augustiniana: Augustine, Second Founder of the Faith*, eds. J.C. Schnaubelt & F. Van Fleteren (New York: Peter Lang, 1990), 421–431; W.S. Babcock, "Augustine on Sin and Moral Agency," *Journal of Religious Ethics* 16 (1988): 28–55.

10   G.R. Evans, *Augustine on Evil* (Cambridge: Cambridge University Press, 1982; reprint, 1991) (subsequent page references are to the reprint edition); G. Sfameni Gasparro, "Natura e origine del male: alle radici dell'incontro e del confronto di Agostino con la gnosi manichea," in *Il mistero del male e la libertà possibile,* Lettura dei Dialoghi di Agostino (Studia Ephemeridis Augustinianum, 45) (Roma: Institutum Patristicum Augustinianum, 1994), 7–55.

11   For a study of the Manichaean understanding of the Good based on Manichaean sources, see J.K. Coyle, "The Idea of the 'Good' in Manichaeism," forthcoming in *Proceedings of the Fourth International Conference on Manichaeism,* Berlin, July 14–18, 1997, ed. W. Sundermann (Berlin: Claudius Naumann), 124–137. Coyle confirms that Augustine has correct understanding although only a partial picture. J. Ries also suggests that Augustine has a good grasp of the Manichaean teachings but only tackles the fundamentals in his apologetics against the Manichees. See J. Ries, "Notes de lecture du *Contra Epistulam Fundamenti* d'Augustin: à la lumière de quelques documents manichéens," *Augustinianum* 35 (1995): 537–548.

12   Unless otherwise stated, all dating of Augustine's works in this study will generally follow the suggestions of O. Perler, *Les voyages de saint Augustin* (Paris: Études Augustiniennes, 1969), 430–477, with reference to the chronological tables of P. Brown, *Augustine of Hippo: A Biography* (Berkeley: University of California Press, 1967), 16, 74–77, 184–187, 282–285, 378–379; E. TeSelle, *Augustine the Theologian,* (London: Burns & Oates, 1970) 11–14; H. Hohensee, *The Augustinian Concept of Authority,* (*Folia,* Supplement II) (New York: Paulist Press, 1954), 5–8; and Coyle, *Augustine's "De Moribus",* 13–16.

Chapter One

1   Unless otherwise stated, the terms "Manichaeism," "Manichaean doctrines," etc. refer to the Roman African version of Manichaeism with which Augustine first came into contact. See p. 6 on **Manichaeism of Roman Africa**.

2   For example, see F. Decret, *Aspects du Manichéisme dans l'Afrique romaine: Les controverses de Fortunatus, Faustus et Félix avec saint Augustin* (Paris: Études Augustiniennes, 1970), 31; P. Alfaric, *L'évolution intellectuelle de saint Augustin* (Paris: E. Nourry, 1918), 216–218; Coyle, *Augustine's "De Moribus"*, 51–52.

3   L.C. Ferrari, "Young Augustine: Both Catholic and Manichee," *Augustinian Studies* 26 (1995): 109–128.

4   Pierre Courcelle observes that the length of time Augustine spent as a Manichaean auditor should be ten years. See P. Courcelle, *Recherches sur les Confessions de saint Augustin*, rev. ed. (Paris: Éditions E. de Boccard, 1968), 78. Nevertheless, Augustine consistently refers to his sojourn in Manichaeism as only extending to nine years. Leo Charles Ferrari has offered some possible solutions to explain this apparent inconsistency. See L.C. Ferrari, "Augustine's 'Nine Years' as a Manichee," *Augustiniana* 25 (1975): 210–216.

5   On the subject of Augustine as a Manichaean auditor, see Brown, *Augustine of Hippo*, 40–114; M. Pellegrino, *Les Confessions de saint Augustin: Guide de lecture* (Paris: Éditions Alsatia, 1960), 83–144; Courcelle, *Recherches*, 60–92; Alfaric, *L'évolution intellectuelle*, 79–225; Coyle, *Augustine's "De Moribus"*, 50–57; Decret, *Aspects du Manichéisme*, 27–38.

6   Despite the dispersion of various Manichaean writings in different regions, only a few titles such as the letters of Mani and *Thesaurus* enjoyed wide circulation. R. Lim, "Unity and Diversity among Western Manichaeans: A Reconsideration of Mani's *sancta ecclesia*," *Revue des études augustiniennes* 35 (1989): 245.

7   For the possible ways Augustine could have acquired knowledge of Manichaeism, see Van Oort, "Augustin und der Manichäismus," 128–135.

8   S.N.C. Lieu, *Manichaeism in the Later Roman Empire and Medieval China*, 2nd rev. ed. (Tübingen: J.C.B. Mohr, 1992), 154–155.

9   See L.C. Ferrari, "Augustine and Astrology," *Laval théologique et philosophique* 33 (1977): 241–243, 247–248.

10   *Idem*, "Astronomy and Augustine's Break with the Manichees," *Revue d'études augustiniennes* 19 (1973): 271.

11   Lieu, *Manichaeism*, 154–155.

12   The solar eclipses occurred on September 8, 378 and January 12, 381. See Ferrari, "Astronomy and Augustine's Break with the Manichees," 272–276. According to Othmar Perler, Augustine would have been teaching at Carthage from 375/6 to 383. Perler, *Voyages*, 133. And since there are no high mountains around Carthage and rain is infrequent in that region, Augustine should have been able to clearly witness both eclipses.

13   Coyle, *Augustine's "De Moribus"*, 56.

14   *Ibid.*, 52.

15   See L.H. Grondijs, "Numidian Manicheism in Augustinus Time," *Nederlands Theologisch Tijdschrift* 9 (1954): 21–42; *idem*, "Analyse du Manichéisme Numidien au IVe siècle," in *Augustinus Magister*, Congrès international

augustinien, Paris, 21–24 septembre 1954, vol. 3 (Paris: Études Augustiniennes, 1954–1955), 391–410. See also L.J. Van der Lof, "Der numidische Manichäismus im vierten Jahrhundert," in *Studia Patristica* 8, papers presented to the Fourth International Conference on Patristic Studies held at Christ Church, Oxford 1963, ed. F.L. Cross, (Texte und Untersuchungen zur Geschichte der altchristlichen Literatur, 93) (Berlin: Akademie-Verlag, 1966), 118–129.

16   F. Decret, "Le manichéisme présentait-il en Afrique et à Rome des particularismes régionaux distinctifs?" *Augustinianum* 34 (1994), 5–40. See also Lim, "Unity and Diversity among Western Manichaeans," 232, n. 4.

17   L.J.R. Ort, *Mani: A Religio-historical Description of his Personality*, (Dissertationes ad Historiam Religionum Pertinentes, 1) (Leiden: E.J. Brill, 1967), 103.

18   See J.J. O'Meara, *The Young Augustine* (London: Longmans Green, 1954), 63; W.H.C. Frend, "The Gnostic-Manichaean Tradition in Roman North Africa," *Journal of Ecclesiastical History* 4 (1953): 21.

19   Grondijs, "Numidian Manichaeism," 22, 25.

20   L.J. Van der Lof, "Mani as the Danger from Persia in the Roman Empire," *Augustiniana* 24 (1974): 82.

21   J.H.S. Burleigh, ed., *Augustine: Earlier Writings*, (The Library of Christian Classics, 6) (London: SCM Press, 1953), 222.

22   R.J. Teske, "*Homo Spiritualis* in St. Augustine's *De Genesi contra Manichaeos*," in *Studia Patristica* 22, papers presented to the Tenth International Conference on Patristic Studies held in Oxford 1987, ed. E.A. Livingstone (Leuven: Peeters Press, 1989), 352.

23   This does not mean, however, that Augustine was the only thinker in the Church to fight against Manichaeism. Besides Ambrose, in the East, there was Ephrem the Deacon and, in the West, there were Serapion of Thmuis, Titus of Bostra, Epiphanius of Salamis and Marius Victorinus (Coyle, *Augustine's "De Moribus"*, 10–13). Other Christian leaders came on the scene a little later like Porphry, bishop of Gaza from 395 to 420, and Rabbula, bishop of Edessa from 412 to 435. See Lieu, *Manichaeism*, 201.

24   *Gen. Man.* I.i.1 (AB, 3 = PL, 34, col. 173): "[...] errores illos tam perniciosos ab animis etiam imperitorum expellere [...]." (All translations of Latin texts cited in this study are my own.)

25   For instance, Honoratus remained a Manichee yet detested the absurdity of Manichaeism from the very beginning (*util.* i.2).

26   See F. Decret, *L'Afrique manichéenne, IVe – Ve siècles: Étude historique et doctrinale*, 2 vols. (Paris: Études Augustiniennes, 1978), 218–219.

27   In Possidius' biography of Augustine, Felix is said to have been converted to Christianity (Lieu, *Manichaeism*, 198). Decret, however, has argued that the Felix who denounced Manichaeism and became a Christian is not the same person who debated with Augustine (*Aspects du Manichéisme*, 333–336). Nevertheless, based on the evidence of textual coherence of a fragment concerning the conversion of

Felix published by Baronius and Mai, Judith Lieu and Samuel Lieu were able to maintain that there was only one converted Felix involved, the one who debated with Augustine. J. Lieu & S. Lieu, "'Felix Conversus ex Manichaeis': A Case of Mistaken Identity," *Journal of Theological Studies* 32 (1981) 173–176, reprinted in Samuel N.C. Lieu, *Manichaeism in Mesopotamia and the Roman East*, (Religions in the Graeco-Roman World, 118) (Leiden: E.J. Brill, 1994), 153–155.

28 See Decret, *L'Afrique manichéenne*, 226–227.

29 *Nat. bon.* xlviii (CSEL, 25/2, 888): "praesta nobis, da nobis, ut per nostrum ministerium, quo execrabilem et nimis horribilem hunc errorem redargui uoluisti, sicut iam multi liberati sunt, et alii liberentur [...]." PL, 42, col. 572 uses "dona nobis" instead of "da nobis," but the two have essentially the same meaning here.

30 J.D. BeDuhn, "A Regimen for Salvation: Medical Models in Manichaean Asceticism," *Semeia* 58 (1992): 126.

31 Augustine does not specifically mention the senses of touch and sound, but they are generally included in his mention of the five senses (*util.* i.1) and of other sensory organs apart from eyes, nostrils and palate (*Faus.* XXXII.20).

32 Incidentally, judgment by the criterion of like or dislike instead of by the true value of things is what Plotinus refers to as the condition of the Soul at fault when serving evil (*Enn.* I.viii.4).

33 In looking for the source of evil, the Manichees have assumed that they already know the nature of evil. But this is where Augustine believes they have erred (*mor.* II.ii.2). To cite carefully chosen difficult biblical passages and then ask Whence comes evil? seems to be a very effective way to make Manichaean converts out of those with some exposure to Christianity (*ago.* iv.4).

34 The term *memoria* here does not mean memory in the usual sense but is synonymous with *animus* (*conf.* IV.xv.24). Hence, it may bear the modern idea of consciousness. See A. Solignac, "Introduction et Notes," in *Oeuvres de saint Augustin*, vol. 14: *Les Confessions: Livres VIII–XIII*, (Bibliothèque augustinienne, 2e série: Dieu et son oeuvre) (Paris: Desclée de Brouwer, 1962), 558–567.

35 That is why Augustine tries to differentiate between the Holy Spirit being borne over the water at the beginning of creation, and the sun through stretches of space being borne over the earth (*Gen. Man.* I.v.8). Besides, since extension in space is a quality belonging only to the body (*Faus.* XXV.2), Augustine argues that the Manichees are thinking of divine substance as body (*corpus*) which, according to the Manichaean theory, must come from the race of darkness (*Faus.* XX.11). Augustine cannot accept any idea of God being corporeal even were this to mean composed of air (*aerium*) or ether (*aetherium*) (*fund.* xv).

36 Augustine thinks that the property of all things which are spatially extended is that they cannot be everywhere simultaneously (*fund.* xix).

37 Augustine's alternative to an "extensional" God is an "intentional" God who is non-extended in time and space.

38 Note that in Augustine's classification of beings, while God is non-extended in both time and space, souls or rational beings including angels are non-extended in

space but extended in time. Even though angels and rational souls are eternal in the sense of being able to enjoy infinitely extended successive time in the future, this eternity is qualitatively different from God's eternity which is above or beyond time altogether. To understand the qualitative transcendence of God, one has to comprehend how one's soul is all at once present everywhere in one's own body (*fund.* xix).

39   Hence, Augustine only admits that the Manichees attempt to go beyond the immediate sense (*uer. rel.* xx.40) yet without success. What they can do is only to recoil from the senses (*recedere a sensibus*) (*util.* i.1).

40   Hence, Augustine's famous saying: "inquietum est cor nostrum, donec requiescat in te" (*conf.* I.i.1).

41   Augustine did not despise asceticism *per se* for he himself was very much attracted to those who could truly practice it. In fact, some *exempla* among the Christians helped psychologically prepare his conversion to the Catholic faith. What Augustine opposed were "the pretensions of the Manichaeans [...] to practice genuine asceticism [...]" (Coyle, *Augustine's "De Moribus"*, 193). The rigorous demands of Manichaean asceticism are once again due to their literalism in their understanding of myth (*ibid.*, 195).

42   Roland J. Teske suggests that Augustine's view of spirituality as an ability to grasp the invisible realities by intellectual insight is Neoplatonic. He further notes the following: "prior to Augustine there was in the whole Western Church no concept of a spiritual reality in the technical sense save in that Neoplatonic circle in the Church of Milan where Augustine heard the sermons of Ambrose, conversed with Theodorus and Simplicianus, and read the *libri Platonicorum*." See Teske, *"Homo Spiritualis,"* 351.

43   Augustine's emphasis on the point that spiritual truths are spiritually discerned makes the Manichaean claim of secret knowledge appear counterfeit (*Gen. Man.* II.xxvi.39, xxvii.41).

44   Augustine's is a trinitarian monism. Coyle notes that Augustine takes the idea that God is incorruptible from Plotinus (cf. *conf.* VII.xx.26) but observes that when Augustine refers to God's immutability, "he almost never uses the shorter forms, *immutabilis* and *inuertibilis*." The use of the longer form *incommutabilis*, according to Coyle, may suggest Augustine's constant awareness of the "trinitarian context" (*Augustine's "De Moribus"*, 332).

45   Prior to Augustine, Plotinus had already raised the issue that the question of nature takes precedence over that of origin. Hence, he says: "Those enquiring whence Evil enters into beings, or rather into a certain order of beings, would be making the best beginning if they established, first of all, what precisely Evil is, what constitutes its Nature" (*Enn.* I.viii.1).

46   Especially in his effort to find an alternate way to explain personal evil, Augustine clearly tries to address the important question of *Unde sit malum?*, but without openly admitting it. See p. 50 on **Alternative explanation of personal evil.**

Chapter Two

1   A.A. Moon, *The De Natura Boni of Saint Augustine: A Translation with an Introduction and Commentary*, (Catholic University of America, Patristic Studies, 88) (Washington: The Catholic University of America Press, 1955), 3, n. 1; S.M. Zarb, *Chronologia Operum S. Augustini: Secundum Ordinem Retractationum Digesta cum Appendice de Operibus in Retractationibus non Recensitis* (Romae: Angelicum, 1934), 44–45; P. Monceaux, *Communication à l'Académie des Inscriptions et Belles-Lettres, Comptes rendus* (Paris, 1908), 51–53 quoted in Zarb, *loc. cit.*

2   See Zarb, *Chronologia*, 8.

3   For the quotation of the original text of Monceaux, see *ibid.*, 13, n. 1.

4   Decret, *Aspects du manichéisme*, 78, n. 2.

5   Le Nain de Tillemont, *Mémoires*, XIII, 413; cited in Decret, *loc. cit.*

6   Moon, *The De Natura Boni*, 4.

7   This assumption may be supported by the title of the work itself, *Epistula Fundamenti*, and the fact that the Manichees are supposed to be familiar with it (*fund.* xxv). See also E. Feldmann, *Die "Epistola Fundamenti" der nordafrikanischen Manichäer: Versuch einer Rekonstruktion* (Altenberge: Akademische Bibliothek, 1987), 1; A.H. Newman, trans., "Against the Epistle of Manichaeus called Fundamental," in *A Selected Library of the Nicene and Post-Nicene Fathers of the Christian Church*, ed. P. Schaff, vol. 4: *St. Augustin: The Writings against the Manichaeans and against the Donatists* (1887; reprint, Grand Rapids: Eerdmans, 1983), 129, n. 1 (page reference is to reprint edition); J. Ries, "Notes de lecture du Contra Epistulam Fundamenti d'Augustin," 547.

8   Cf. Newman, "Against the Epistle of Manichaeus called Fundamental," 129, n. 1.

9   Moon, *The De Natura Boni*, 3.

10 Though both Perler (*Voyages*, 443) and Brown (*Augustine of Hippo*, 184) date the completion of the *Confessiones* at 401, Coyle observes that most authors consider the date to be 400 (*Augustine's "De Moribus"*, 15).

11 *Retr.* II.ix (CC, 57, 97 = PL, 32, col. 634): "Liber de natura boni aduersus Manichaeos est, ubi ostenditur naturam incommutabilem deum esse ac summum bonum, atque ab illo esse ceteras naturas siue spiritales siue corporales, atque omnes, in quantum naturae sunt, bonas esse; et quid uel unde sit malum, et quanta mala Manichaei ponant in natura boni et quanta bona in natura mali, quas naturas finxit error ipsorum."

12 *Faus.* XIII.6 (CSEL, 25/1, 383–384 = PL, 42, cols. 284–285): "fabula illa est longa et uana, puerile ludibrium et muliebre auocamentum et aniculare deliramentum continens initium truncum et medium putridum et finem ruinosum. cum enim uobis ex eius initio dictum fuerit: inmortali, inuisibili, incorruptibili deo quid factura erat gens tenebrarum, si cum ea pugnare noluisset? et de medio eius: quomodo est incorruptibilis et incontaminabilis deus, cuius membra in pomis et oleribus manducando et digerendo conteritis, ut purgetis? et de fine eius: quid fecit anima

misera, ut in globo tenebrarum perpetuo uinculo puniatur, quae non suo uitio, sed alieno maculata deo suo deficiente mundari non potuit, quo mittente polluta est?"

13   *Fel.* II.xiii (CSEL, 25/2, 842 = PL, 42, col. 544): "absit enim a cordibus ueritatem quaerentium uel tenentium, ut credant deum substantiam suam necessitate coactum mersisse daemonum naturae ligandam atque polluendam; absit a fidelibus credere deum ad liberandam substantiam suam conuertere se in masculos contra feminas et in feminas contra masculos ad eorum concupiscentiam inritandam; absit a fidelibus credere deum substantiam suam, quam ipse daemonibus mersit, postea in aeternum damnare."

14   See J.H.S. Burleigh, ed., *Augustine: Earlier Writings*, (The Library of Christian Classics, 6) (London: SCM Press, 1953), 325.

15   See p. 65.

16   *Nat. bon.* xlii (CSEL, 25/2, 877 = PL, 42, col. 565): "Manichaeus apertissime in epistula ruinosi sui Fundamenti delirat. oblitus enim, quod paulo ante dixerat: 'ita autem fundata sunt eiusdem splendidissima regna supra lucidam et beatam terram, ut a nullo umquam aut moueri aut concuti possint', postea dixit: [...]." Compare this with *fund.* xiii, xxviii.

17   *Nat. bon.* xiv (CSEL, 25/2, 860 = PL, 42, col. 555): "Sed in his omnibus quaecumque parua sunt, in maiorum comparatione contrariis nominibus appellantur: sicut in hominis forma quia maior est pulchritudo, in eius comparatione simiae pulchritudo deformitas dicitur. et fallit inprudentes, tamquam illud sit bonum et hoc malum [...]."

18   Other studies on Augustine's concept of aesthetics, see K. Eschweiler, *Die ästhetischen Elemente in der Religionsphilosophie des hl. Augustin*, Inaugural-Dissertation der philosophischen Fakultät (Sektion I) an der Ludwig-Maximilians-Universität München zur Erlangung der Doktorwürde am 11. Juni 1909 vorgelegt, (Euskirchen: Buchdruckerei der Euskirchener Volkszeitung, 1909); see also, T. Manferdini, *L'estetica religiosa in S. Agostino* (Studi e ricerche, N.S., 16) (Bologna: Zanichelli, 1969).

19   Manichaean evil principle that gives form to bodies. See p. 66.

20   *Nat. bon.* xviii (CSEL, 25/2, 862 = PL, 42, col. 557): "si bonum aliquod est forma, unde qui ea praeualent formosi appellantur, sicut a specie speciosi, procul dubio bonum aliquid est etiam capacitas formae [...]."

21   The link between form (*forma*) and beauty (*species*) here is ambiguous (Moon, *The De Natura Boni*, 161). W.J. Roche notes that Augustine's use of *species* is "always obscure, falling between the notions of form and beauty, almost as if the two were identical." W.J. Roche, "Measure, Number and Weight in Saint Augustine," *The New Scholasticism* 15 (1941): 355. That may be the price Augustine has to pay to put the Neoplatonic idea into Manichaean garb.

22   E. Chapman, *Saint Augustine's Philosophy of Beauty*, (Saint Michael's Mediaeval Studies. Monograph series) (New York: Sheed & Ward, 1939), 56. Also, Augustín Uña Juárez, "*Pulchritudinis leges*: Interioridad y orden en el ejemplarismo estético de san Agustín," *La Ciudad Dios* 208 (1998): 849–882; *idem*, "San Agustín ante la belleza: Claves de interpretación," *Religión y cultura* 42 (1995): 577–595.

23   *Nat. bon.* xx (CSEL, 25/2, 863 = PL, 42, col. 557): "Dolor autem, quod praecipue malum nonnulli arbitrantur, siue in animo sit siue in corpore, [...]."

24   The Manichaean idea that whatever is hurtful is evil is stated most explicitly by Augustine in *mor.* II.ix.16.

25   See p. 65.

26   *Nat. bon.* xli (CSEL, 25/2, 875 = PL, 42, col. 564): "[...] dicunt [...] et sensisse se inuicem ac sibi uicinum lumen, et oculos habuisse, quibus illud longe conspicerent [...], et suauitate suae uoluptatis esse perfruitos [...]. Nisi autem etiam qualiscumque pulchritudo ibi fuisset, nec amarent coniugia sua nec partium congruentia corpora eorum constarent; [...]. et nisi pax aliqua ibi esset, principi suo non oboedirent."

27   C.R.C. Allberry, ed., *A Manichaean Psalm-Book*, Part II, with a contribution by H. Ibscher, (Manichaean Manuscripts in the Chester Beatty Collection, 2) (Stuttgart: W. Kohlhammer, 1938), 166, ll. 6–9.

28   Augustine picks up the Manichaean notion of peace as inner tranquility and further develops it as his basic philosophical concept of "the tranquility of order" (cf. *ciu. dei* XIX.xiii.1). See Moon, *The De Natura Boni*, 197–198.

29   *Nat. bon.* ii (CSEL, 25/2, 856= PL, 42, col. 552): "[...] mouentur spiritus iniquitate et corporis mortalitate et ob hoc aliam naturam maligni spiritus et mortalis corporis, quam deus non fecerit, conantur inducere [...]." See also Moon, *The De Natura Boni*, 125.

30   See also Moon, *De Natura Boni*, 138, 167.

31   *Nat. bon.* xx (CSEL, 25/2, 863 = PL, 42, col. 557): "Sunt autem mala sine dolore peiora; peius est enim gaudere de iniquitate quam dolere de corruptione."

32   Cf. James J. O'Donnell, *Augustine: Confessions*, vol. 2: *Commentary on Books 1–7* (Oxford: Clarendon Press, 1992), 247.

33   There are at least two instances of this continuity: the continuous framework of "happy life" (*beata uita*) (see p. 31) and Augustine's reference to "suitability" (*aptus*) in *De ordine* (see p. 68).

34   Coyle, *Augustine's "De Moribus"*, 56.

35   B. Roland-Gosselin traces Augustine's idea of beatitude to Cicero and Seneca. B. Roland-Gosselin, "Notes complémentaires aux *De moribus ecclesiae catholicae et de moribus manichaeorum*," in *Oeuvres de saint Augustin*, vol. 1: *La morale chrétienne: De moribus ecclesiae catholicae et de moribus manichaeorum, De agone christiano, De natura boni*, (Bibliothèque augustinienne, 1re série: Opuscules) (Paris: Desclée de Brouwer, 1949), 515. Nevertheless, this does not exclude the possibility of a Manichaean influence on Augustine. It is likely that Augustine, as is true with many of his other ideas, forms his own notion of happy life by drawing from a variety of sources and Manichaean inspiration is one of them.

36   It is generally recognized that Augustine is attempting an ascent in *De puchro et apto*. E.g., O'Donnell, *Confessions*, vol. 2, 255–256. M. Testard observes that this

early work is Augustine's attempt to use the analogical method to arrive at the ultimate truth by ascending from material bodies. M. Testard, *Saint Augustin et Cicéron* (Paris: Études augustiniennes, 1958), 51, n. 1. This method of inquiry continues to be employed after Augustine's conversion until the writing of *De uera religione* (390). See also F. Van Fleteren, "The Cassiciacum Dialogues and Augustine's Ascents at Milan," *Mediaevalia* 4 (1978): 59.

37   *Conf.* IV.xv.27 (CC, 27/1, 54 = PL, 32, col. 704): "stare cupiens et audire te et gaudere propter uocem sponsi (Jn. 3:29) [...]."

38   See p. 20.

39   Cf. O'Donnell, *Confessions*, vol. 2, 258.

40   *Conf.* IV.xiii.20 (CC, 25/1, 50–51 = PL, 32, col. 701): "Num amamus aliquid nisi pulchrum? Quid est ergo pulchrum? Et quid est pulchritudo? Quid est quod nos allicit et conciliat rebus, quas amamus? Nisi enim esset in eis decus et species, nullo modo nos ad se mouerent."

41   D.A. Cress, "Hierius & St. Augustine's Account of the Lost *De Pulchro et Apto*: *Confessions* IV, 13–15," *Augustinian Studies* 7 (1976): 162.

42   Augustine's demythologization process is probably helped by the Aristotelian idea of Supreme Good. Aristotle identifies Supreme Good with "happiness," which is attained through intellectual contemplation. See Book One of Aristotle's *Nicomachean Ethics*.

43   Takeshi Katô has convincingly argued for a direct or indirect influence on *De pulchro et apto* from a Manichaean source ("*Melodia interior*: sur le traité *De pulchro et apto*," *Revue des études augustiniennes* 12 [1966]: 229–240), and most commentators do not deny it except Jean-Michel Fontanier who objects to the idea on two counts. First, Katô's citations from the fragments of *Médînêt Mâdî* regarding the theme of beauty do not reflect Augustine's notions of *pulchrum* and *aptum* (*ibid.*, 231–233). Second, *conf.* III.vii.13 shows that the illustration of "shoe fitting" is used as a refutation against Manichaean critiques of the immoralities of the Old Testament; hence, its employment in *conf.* IV.xiii.20 should also reflect his anti-Manichaean attitude. J.-M. Fontanier, "Sur le traité d'Augustin *De pulchro et apto*: Convenance, beauté et adaptation," *Revue des sciences philosophiques et théologiques* 73 (1989): 413–414. To answer the first objection, we need to ask why "beauty," that which is judged by the senses, is chosen as the route of inquiry (*conf.* IV.xiii.20), if sensible objects—even a divine shining body (xvi.31)—were not in Augustine's mind. Moreover, "beauty" is a common theme in Manichaean literature (Katô, "*Melodia interior*," 231–233). Fontanier doubts the Manichaean influence because the texts cited by Katô do not seem to reflect Augustine's notions of *pulchrum* and *aptum* ("Traité d'Augustin," 413). Nonetheless, Fontanier's objection does not preclude the Manichaean influence as a motivation for Augustine's choice of the issue of "beauty" as the route of inquiry. Fontanier's second objection is not well grounded because the meaning of an illustration should also be sought in the immediate context, though there may be similarities in all its applications.

44   Karel Svoboda notes that Augustine "a à peine entendu parler de l'*Hippias* de Platon, dialogue auquel son exposé correspond le plus, car c'est un ouvrage qu'on

ne lisait guère" (*L'esthétique de saint Augustin et ses sources* [Brno: A. Pisa, 1933], 13).

45   Cress, "Hierius," 157.

46   Fontanier, "Traité d'Augustin," 414–416.

47   The same illustration, however, is also found in *Hippias Major* 294a (*ibid.*, 414).

48   Testard, *Saint Augustin et Cicéron*, 61.

49   Fontanier, "Traité d'Augustin," 416–418.

50   Solignac suggests: "Il est fort possible, et presque certain, qu'Augustin a connu ces thèmes platoniciens par la tradition des écoles de rhétorique, tandis qu'il pouvait connaître Cicéron par une étude directe; cependant il présente une systématisation bien personnelle" (*Les Confessions: Livres VIII–XIII*, 671).

51   See pp. 37f.

52   Augustine recalls that in the process of his writing, the bodily figments wind around him and pound on his heart (*conf.* xv.27).

53   W. Eborowicz observes that Plotinus' fundamental qualifications of the Absolute consist of "the One" and "the Good." W. Eborowicz, *La contemplation selon Plotin*, (Biblioteca del 'Giornale di metafisica,' 14) (Torino: Societa Editrice Internazionale, 1958), 39, 42. Augustine here is applying the Plotinian frame to his Manichaean theme of beauty.

54   Svoboda observes that *monad* and *dyad* are terms used by the Academics who based their reasoning on Plato's Pythagorean doctrine of two principles of the world (*L'esthétique*, 15).

55   See also *ibid.*, 14. Although some scholars believe that Augustine may have borrowed the idea of *summum bonum* or Supreme Good from Cicero (cf. *Tusc.* v.37ff), this opinion can hardly be conclusive because the same idea appears also in Manichaeism (e.g., *nat. bon.* ii). See Mayer, et al., eds. *Augustinus-Lexikon*, s.v. "Bonum," by N. Fischer; also F. Van Fleteren, "Augustine's *De vera religione*: A New Approach," *Augustinianum* 16 (1976): 494. It seems clear that the notion originates from Plato's *agathou idéa* (*Rep.* VI), "which is the source of all truth, all goodness, and all beauty." J. Hastings, ed., *Encyclopaedia of Religion and Ethics*, vol. 6, (Edinburgh: T. & T. Clark, 1914), s.v. "Goodness," by J. Strahan; also M. Eliade, et al., eds., *The Encyclopedia of Religion*, vol. 6, (New York: MacMillan, 1987), s.v. "Good, The," by L. Kolakowski. Yet, it is possible that in Augustine's time *summum bonum* has become a common idea with different shades of meaning according to various schools of thought. Thus, Augustine as well as the Manichees also drew on the idea and added their nuances to it.

Chapter Three

1   *Nat. bon.* i (CSEL, 25/2, 855 = PL, 42, col. 551): "Summum bonum, quo superius non est, deus est; ac per hoc incommutabile bonum est; ideo uere aeternum et uere inmortale."

2   For an explanation of these terms, see Moon, *De Natura Boni*, 126–128.

3   *Nat. bon.* xxii (CSEL, 25/2, 864 = PL, 42, col. 558): "Deus autem nec modum habere dicendus est, ne finis eius dici putetur. nec ideo tamen immoderatus est, a quo modus omnibus rebus tribuitur, ut aliquo modo esse possint. nec rursum moderatum oportet dici deum, tamquam ab aliquo modum acceperit. si autem dicamus eum summum modum, forte aliquid dicimus, si tamen in eo, quod dicimus summum modum, intellegamus summum bonum. omnis enim modus, in quantum modus est, bonus est: unde omnia moderata, modesta, modificata dici sine laude non possunt [...]."

4   Coyle argues that *De Genesi contra Manichaeos* was written between the composition of the two books of the *De moribus* (*Augustine's "De Moribus"*, 66–79).

5   O. Du Roy, *L'intelligence de la foi en la Trinité selon saint Augustin: Genèse de sa théologie trinitaire jusqu'en 391* (Paris: Études Augustiniennes, 1966), 279–281; also C. Harrison, "Measure, Number and Weight in Saint Augustine's Aesthetics," *Augustinianum* 28 (1988): 591–602.

6   The second point comes from Stoicism. See Coyle, *Augustine's "De Moribus"*, 319–320.

7   The concept of "love for" the Supreme Good has a Plotinian origin (Eborowicz, *La contemplation selon Plotin*, 48–49, 59) whereas the "enjoyment of" it has an undertone of the Manichaean idea of aesthetic pleasure. By linking the two notions, Augustine is trying to fit his "Manichaean" approach to the Plotinian vehicle. See pp. 37f. The Manichaean undertone in Augustine's reference to "enjoyment" is suggested by his attempt to connect the notion of "enjoyment" to "beauty" in *beat. uit.* ii.8 (see p. 34).

8   See p. 34.

9   See p. 23.

10   In writing the anti-Manichaean treatises, Augustine has two groups of people in mind. To the first group belong the inexperienced Catholics who, lacking firm grounding in the faith, were easily enticed by Manichaean teachings (e.g., Romanianus, *uer. rel.* vii.12). To the second group belong the Manichees deemed convertible, some of whom may even be Augustine's former friends (*duab. anim.* xiv.23–xv.24; *util.* i.2). Augustine's address sometimes switches from one group to another. For instance, *mor.* II.xv.36–xvi.38 treats the Manichees in the third person whereas they are addressed directly as second person before and after. Augustine's primary concern is not to convert the obstinate Manichees but to stem the tide of Manichaeism which was damaging the Catholic Church. See also p. 7.

11   See also J. Doignon, "Notes complémentaires," in *Oeuvres de saint Augustin*, vol. 4/1: *Dialogues philosophiques: De beata vita—La vie heureuse*, rev. ed. (Bibliothèque augustinienne, 1re série: Opuscules) (Paris: Desclée de Brouwer, 1986), 135.

12   There may be two possible understandings of *beata uita*. In the general sense, it is a happy life desired by all. But more specifically, it can be understood as a blessed life when one has God in possession. In *De beata uita*, both senses are present.

Augustine starts with the general sense but ends with the specific sense at the final stage of the ascent when the quality of happiness is transformed into beatitude. Furthermore, the relation between *beata uita* and *bonum* is developed in the treatise in three stages: 1) everyone has the *desire* to be happy, 2) a happy life derives from having *good desire*, and 3) happiness is to *desire the good*. L.F. Pizzolato, "Il *De beata vita* o la possibile felicità nel tempo," in *L'opera letteraria di Aogostino tra Cassiciacum e Milano*, Agostino nelle terre di Ambrogio (1–4 ottobre 1986), eds. G. Reale, et al. (Palermo: Edizioni Augustinus, 1987), 88.

13   The first two Cassiciacum dialogues, *Contra academicos* and *De beata uita*, were composed in the same year (386). The two are logically related in reflecting the mind of the young convert. Although *Contra academicos*, according to the record of *Retractationes*, was begun before *De beata uita*, the latter is judged to have logical priority over the former. Van Fleteren, "Cassiciacum Dialogues," 60. As recalled in *De beata uita* and recorded in *Contra academicos*, Augustine's concern with the Academics is about the certainty of truth as the foundation for happy life (*beat. uit.* ii.13–15; *acad.* I.ii.5–iv.12, ix.24–25).

14   By "Platonic concept," we do not necessarily imply that at 380 when *De pulchro et apto* was written Augustine has read Plato or Neoplatonic works. Rather, Augustine could have been exposed to some form of Platonic idea of order indirectly through others, such as Cicero (see p. 24).

15   *Acad.* II.iii.7 (CC, 29, 21 = PL, 32, col. 922): "[...] philocalia et philosophia prope similiter cognominatae sunt et quasi gentiles inter se uideri uolunt et sunt. Quid est enim philosophia? amor sapientiae. Quid philocalia? amor pulchritudinis. Quaere de Graecis. Quid ergo sapientia? nonne ipsa uera est pulchritudo? Germanae igitur istae prorsus et eodem parente procreatae; sed illa uisco libidinis detracta caelo suo et inclusa cauea populari uiciniam tamen nominis tenuit ad commonendum aucupem, ne illam contemnat. Hanc igitur sine pennis sordidatam et egentem uolitans libere soror saepe agnoscit, sed raro liberat; non enim philocalia ista unde genus ducat, agnoscit nisi philosophia."

16   See p. 10.

17   A clear example of this parallelism between physical beauty and spiritual wisdom can also be found in *conf.* XIII.ii.3.

18   The very notion of measure was not foreign to the ancient Greeks. Augustine borrowed this idea through Cicero's adaptation (E.B.J. Postma, *Augustinus De Beata Vita* [Amsterdam: H.J. Paris, 1946], 169). Doignon has identified the source of the concept "wisdom as measure." It came from Cicero's *Tusculanae* 3, 8, 16 (*De beata vita—La vie heureuse*, 148). Pizzolato shows the path through which the two ideas connect: "la felicità è sapienza (postulato di base); la sapienza è *plenitudo*; la *plenitudo* è *frugalitas* (in quanto rientra nell'orizzonte dell'*esse*); la *frugalitas* è *modus*; quindi la sapienza/felicità è *modus*" ("Il *De beata vita*," 94–95).

19   The idea of keeping an equilibrium of the soul takes its origin from Cicero's *Tusculanae* 4, 6, 11–14. Doignon, *De beata vita—La vie heureuse*, 148.

20   The development of the idea of nurture of the soul in ancient philosophy has a complex history (*ibid.*, 141).

21   L.F. Pizzolato, "Il *modus* nel primo Agostino," in *La langue latine, langue de la philosophie* (Collection de l'Ecole Française Rome, 161) (Rome: 1992), 248.

22   Indeed, having analyzed the usage of the word, Steven Barbone believes that Augustine's meaning of *frugalitas* "refers to a principle of ordering or appropriateness which sets limits, not only for things negative such as vice, passion, or appetite, but also for those good qualities such as virtue." S. Barbone, "*Frugalitas* in Saint Augustine," *Augustiniana* 44 (1994): 15. See also pp. 37–38, the section on **Plotinian Vehicle for a Manichaean Notion**.

23   These two considerations are in accordance with the two stages of questioning in Augustine's disputation on the happy life regarding the qualifications of the object to be possessed (ii.10–11) and the subject which possesses this object (iii.17).

24   S. MacDonald sees the notion of fulfillment or actualization of created nature within its given measure as a kind of *internal account* that gives Augustine's theory of goodness as existence self-authentication ("Augustine's Christian-Platonist Account of Goodness," 507).

25   Postma has determined that Augustine's idea of fullness (*plenitudo*) comes from Plotinus (*Enn.* I.iv.6). Especially in V.vi.6, Plotinus pointed out that what distinguishes real beings is not merely their unchangeable self-identical existence by their essence but their fullness of being. Postma, *Augustinus*, 167–168. Moreover, it is due to the influence of Cicero's concept of *frugalitas* that Augustine links *plenitudo* to *modestia* and *temperantia* but contrasts it with *abundantia*. Doignon, *De beata vita—La vie heureuse*, 147–148.

26   Augustine's notion of *summus modus* betrays his use of a Plotinian vehicle. Plotinus removes the idea of limit and measure which would otherwise apply to created things and he does so, not by simple negation but by both affirmation and negation. Eborowicz, *La contemplation selon Plotin*, 40–41. See also Doignon, *De beata vita—La vie heureuse*, 149.

27   J. Doignon, "Augustin, *De beata vita* 4,34: *Sapientia dei* est-elle une appellation impersonnelle?" in *De Tertullien aux Mozarabes: Antiquité tardive et christianisme ancien (IIIe–VIe siècles): Mélanges offerts à Jacques Fontaine*, eds. L. Holtz & J.-C. Fredouille (Paris: Études Augustinniennes, 1992), 151–155.

28   Du Roy thinks that it is the Spirit, not the Son, who is emanating and returning to the Source of Truth (Du Roy, *L'intelligence de la foi*, 161–162), but this view is questionable because the identity of the third person at this point is far from clear. Du Roy may have assumed the full trinitarian structure (cf. *ibid.*, 161: "l'Esprit mène à la Sagesse et celle-ci mène au Père") and read it back into the text.

29   *Beat. uit.* iv.35 (CC, 29, 84 = PL, 32, col. 976): "pie perfecteque cognoscere, a quo inducaris in ueritatem, qua ueritate perfruaris, per quid conectaris summo modo." There is no scholarly consensus as to the exact identification of the three persons of the Trinity (Doignon, *De beata vita—La vie heureuse*, 151–152). Hence, the question whether the passage provides an explicit trinitarian identification is far from settled.

30   See n. 18 of this chapter.

31   See n. 26 of this chapter.

32　For Plotinus, contemplation and love are closely related (Eborowicz, *La contemplation selon Plotin*, 59). Hence, Plotinus recounts the experience of contemplating this supreme Beauty: "And one that shall know this vision—with what passion of love shall he not be seized, with what pang of desire, what longing to be molten into one with This, what wondering delight! If he that has never seen this Being must hunger for It as for all his welfare, he that has known must love and reverence It as the very Beauty; he will be flooded with awe and gladness, stricken by a salutary terror; he loves with a veritable love, with sharp desire; all other loves than this he must despise, and disdain all that once seemed fair" (*Enn.* I.vi.7). By comparison, the language Augustine used in the account of the experience he shared with his mother at Ostia seems tame (*conf.* IX.x.23–26).

33　See n. 7 of this chapter.

34　C. Harrison, *Beauty and Revelation in the Thought of Saint Augustine* (Oxford: Clarendon Press, 1992), 4–5.

35　See p. 25.

36　Eborowicz identifies these aspects of contemplative experience in Plotinus (*La contemplation selon Plotin*, 58–64).

37　See p. 34.

38　At about this time when *De natura boni* was composed, Augustine explicitly identified that God is the Beauty (*conf.* X.xxvii.38). That means that God is the ground of all beautiful things. See J. Kreuzer, *Pulchritudo: Vom Erkennen Gottes bei Augustin Bemerkungen zu den Büchern IX, X und XI der 'Confessiones'* (München: Wilhelm Fink Verlag, 1995), 3–4.

39　This is, of course, done through the Plotinian vehicle. See Harrison, *Beauty and Revelation*, 36–39.

40　*Ibid.*, 39–40.

41　See p. 67.

42　*Mensura et numerus et pondus* (*nat. bon.* xxi) is equivalent to *modus, species, et ordo* (iii). See Du Roy, *L'intelligence de la foi*, 279–281; Harrison, "Measure, Number and Weight," 591–602.

Chapter Four

1　On the discussion of Augustine's understanding of the issue of the two souls, see Decret, *L'Afrique manichéenne*, 325–336; U. Bianchi, "Sur la question des deux âmes de l'homme dans le manichéisme," in *A Green Leaf*, papers in honour of Professor Jes P. Asmussen, ed. J. Duchesne-Guillemin, (Acta Iranica, 28; Hommages et Opera Minora, 12) (Leiden: E.J. Brill, 1988), 311–316; R. Ferwerda, "Two Souls: Origen's and Augustine's Attitude Toward the Two Souls Doctrine, its Place in Greek and Christian Philosophy." *Vigiliae Christianae* 37 (1983): 360–378; Coyle, *Augustine's "De Moribus"*, 41–42, n. 184.

2   Van Oort, "Augustine on Sexual Concupiscence," 382–386; *idem*, "Augustine and Mani on Concupiscentia Sexualis," 137–152; Babcock, "Augustine on Sin and Moral Agency," 28–55. Babcock asserts that Augustine "never quite managed to shed his Manichaean past" (*ibid.*, 30). In part, this study attempts to move Babcock's theory forward by substantiating his claim.

3   J. Pelikan, *The Christian Tradition: A History of the Development of Doctrine*, vol. 1: *The Emergence of the Catholic Tradition (100–600)* (Chicago: The University of Chicago Press, 1971), 280.

4   Van Oort, "Augustine and Mani on Concupiscentia Sexualis," 151.

5   *Consuetudo* is generally translated as "habit" but since Augustine's usage cannot be fully represented by the term, we leave it untranslated in most part of our discussion.

6   Augustine's attempt is noted also by J. Pegon in "Notes complémentaires au *De vera religione*," in *Oeuvres de saint Augustin*, vol. 8: *La foi chrétienne: De vera religione, De utilitate credendi, De fide rerum quae non videntur, De fide et operibus*, (Bibliothèque augustinienne, 1re série: Opuscules) (Paris: Desclée de Brouwer, 1951), 476.

7   J.G. Prendiville, "Development of the Idea of Habit in the Thought of Saint Augustine," *Traditio* 28 (1972): 31–33.

8   *Mor.* I.xxii.40 (CSEL, 90, 45–46 = PL, 32, col. 1328): "Amor [...] quem tota sanctitate inflammatum esse oportet in deum, in non appetendis istis temperans, in amittendis fortis uocatur. Sed inter omnia quae in hac uita possidentur, corpus homini grauissimum est uinculum iustissimis dei legibus propter antiquum peccatum, quo nihil est ad praedicandum notius, nihil ad intelligendum secretius. Hoc ergo uinculum ne concutiatur atque uexetur, laboris et doloris, ne auferatur autem atque perimatur mortis terrore animam quatit. Amat enim illud ui consuetudinis, non intelligens, si eo bene atque scienter utatur, resurrectionem reformationemque eius ope ac lege diuina sine ulla molestia iuri suo subditam fore [...]."

9   *Gen. Man.* II.xix.29 (AB, 29 = PL, 34, col. 211): "nulla abstinentia fit a uoluntate carnali, quae non habeat in exordio dolorem, donec in meliorem partem consuetudo flectatur. Quod cum prouenerit, quasi natus est filius, id est ad bonum opus paratus affectus per consuetudinem bonam. Quae consuetudo ut nasceretur, cum dolore reluctatum est consuetudini malae."

10 Although the ideas are already present at this early stage, these two terms do not actually appear until *lib. arb.* III.xviii.52, possibly around 395. J. Doignon observes that the idea of *ignorantia et difficultas* might be influenced by Cicero and Virgil. The expression itself reflects Cicero's couplet of *errores et aerumnae*. J. Doignon, "Souvenirs cicéroniens (Hortensius, Consolation) et virgiliens dans l'exposé d'Augustin sur l'état humain d'"ignorance et de difficulté' (Aug., lib. arb. 3, 51–54)," *Vigiliae Christianae* 47 (1993): 132.

11 J. Wetzel, "The Recovery of Free Agency in the Theology of St. Augustine," *Harvard Theological Review* 80 (1987): 114–115. Wetzel does not explain how *consuetudo* works to obstruct a character change. In fact, he seems to avoid the issue of the inevitability of personal evil as he shies away from the question of

original sin (*ibid.*, 124). In this chapter, we attempt to address the issue of constriction of character change by exploring how bodily corruption bears on the soul in terms of both moral difficulty and ignorance. See pp. 47–50, the section on **Penalty as mortality redefined**.

12 See p. 49.

13 *Uer. rel.* iii.3 (CC, 32, 189 = PL, 34, col. 124): "dum nascentium atque transeuntium rerum amore ac dolore sauciatur et dedita consuetudini huius uitae atque sensibus corporis inanibus uanescit imaginibus [...]."

14 See p. 48.

15 See p. 21.

16 Prior to *De uera religione,* the term *nequitia* was mentioned only in *De beata uita,* but it is here that the idea of personal evil becomes the issue.

17 The dual term of "sin" and "penalty" appears earlier in *Gen. Man.* II.ix.12 (cf. *lib. arb.* I.i.1), where sin is attributed to pride and moral difficulty is subsequently experienced as punishment. The frequency of occurrence of the pair or its equivalent, however, increases dramatically only in *De uera religione* (e.g., xii.23, xv.29, xvi.32, xx.39, xxi.41, xxiii.44, xl.76).

18 *Uer. rel.* xi.21 (CC, 32, 200 = PL, 34, col. 131): "nec aliqua uita, in quantum uita est, malum est, sed in quantum uergit ad mortem. Mors autem uitae non est nisi nequitia, quae ab eo quod nequiquam sit dicta est, et ideo nequissimi homines nihili homines appellantur. Uita ergo uoluntario defectu deficiens ab illo, qui eam fecit et cuius essentia fruebatur, et uolens contra dei legem frui corporibus, quibus eam deus praefecit, uergit ad nihilum. Et haec est nequitia, non quia corpus iam nihil est [...]."

19 This double aspect of penal suffering is first found in *De Genesi contra Manichaeos* where Augustine believes that humankind has lost perfection in the fall and become mortal as a result of sinning (xviii.29; II.xxvi.38). Other than physical death, fallen human beings are consigned to struggle with irrational emotions (cf. I.xix.30) which they must control with all the energy they have (xx.31).

20 *Uer. rel.* xii.23 (CC, 32, 202 = PL, 34, col. 132): "Trahitur ergo ad poenas, quia diligendo inferiora in egestate uoluptatum suarum et in doloribus apud inferos ordinatur. Quid est enim dolor qui dicitur corporis, nisi corruptio repentina salutis eius rei, quam male utendo anima corruptioni obnoxiauit? Quid autem dolor qui dicitur animi, nisi carere mutabilibus rebus, quibus fruebatur aut frui se posse sperauerat?"

21 In an earlier sentence in *uer. rel.* xii.23, Augustine's mention of disobedience of God's precept regarding the command and prohibition of eating and not eating evidently refers to the fall in Eden.

22 See p. 51.

23 *Uer. rel.* xiii.26 (CC, 32, 203–204 = PL, 34, col. 133): "ea uoluntate, qua magis deum quam se diligunt, firmi et stabiles manent in illo et fruuntur maiestate ipsius ei uni libentissime subditi. Ille autem angelus magis se ipsum quam deum

diligendo subditus ei esse noluit et intumuit per superbiam et a summa essentia defecit et lapsus est. Et ob hoc minus est quam fuit, quia eo quod minus erat frui uoluit, cum magis uoluit sua potentia frui quam dei. Quamquam enim non summe, tamen amplius erat, quando eo quod summe est fruebatur, quoniam deus solus summe est. Quidquid autem minus est quam erat, non in quantum est, sed in quantum minus est malum est. Eo enim, quo minus est quam erat, tendit ad mortem. Quid autem mirum, si ex defectu inopia et ex inopia inuidentia, qua diabolus utique diabolus est?"

24   Evans, *Augustine on Evil*, 36.

25   *Uer. rel.* xxi.41 (CC, 32, 212–213 = PL, 34, col. 139): "Temporalium enim specierum multiformitas ab unitate dei hominem lapsum per carnales sensus diuerberauit et mutabili uarietate multiplicauit eius affectum. Ita facta est abundantia laboriosa et si dici potest copiosa egestas, dum aliud et aliud sequitur et nihil cum eo permanet."

26   Evans, *Augustine on Evil*, 38.

27   See p. 35.

28   See p. 48.

29   By carefully employing the concept of corruption, Augustine has opened a way for the operation of grace to help fallen humans out of the vicious circle, or, to put it differently, to break loose from the seeming inevitability of personal evil.

30   *Duab. anim.* xiii.19 (CSEL, 25/1, 76 = PL, 42, col. 108): "Neque enim nullo in subplicio sumus peccato transgressionis mortales ex inmortalibus facti. Eo contingit, ut cum ad meliora conantibus nobis consuetudo facta cum carne et peccata nostra quodam modo militare contra nos et difficultatem nobis facere coeperint [...]."

31   See also *uer. rel.* xx.40 where the struggle is considered to be due to the carnal mind, and the expression *consuetudo carnalis* (xlvi.88) discussed, respectively, in p. 49 and p. 45.

32   *Fort.* 22 (CSEL, 25/1, 103–104 = PL, 42, col. 124): "Liberum uoluntatis arbitrium in illo homine fuisse dico, qui primus formatus est. Ille sic factus est, ut nihil omnino uoluntati eius resisteret, si uellet dei praecepta seruare. Postquam autem libera ipse uoluntate peccauit, nos in neccessitatem praecipitati sumus, qui ab eius stirpe descendimus. Potest autem unusquisque nostrum mediocri consideratione inuenire uerum esse, quod dico. Hodie namque in actionibus nostris antequam consuetudine aliqua inplicemur, librum habemus arbitrium faciendi aliquid uel non faciendi. Cum autem ista libertate fecerimus aliquid et facti ipsius tenuerit animam perniciosa dulcedo et uoluptas, eadem ipsa consuetudine sua sic inplicatur, ut postea uincere non possit, quod sibi ipsa peccando fabricata est."

33   See p. 49.

34   J.P. Burns, *The Development of Augustine's Doctrine of Operative Grace* (Paris: Études Augustiniennes, 1980), 24, n. 56.

35   Prendiville, "Development of the Idea of Habit," 68–69; also Brown, *Augustine of Hippo*, 149.

36   P.L. Fredriksen, "Augustine's Early Interpretation of Paul" (Ph.D. diss., Princeton University, 1979), 105.

37   E.g., *exp. Rom.* 29:37, 37:44.

38   Babcock, "Sin and Moral Agency," 39–40.

39   Van Oort, "Augustine and Mani on Concupiscentia Sexualis," 140–152; *idem*, "Augustine on Sexual Concupiscence," 382–386.

40   *Thesaurus Linguae Latinae*, editus auctoritate et consilio academiarum quinque Germanicarum Berolensis, Gottingensis, Lipsiensis, Monacensis, Vidobonensis, vol. 4 (Lipsiae: B.G. Teubneri, 1906–1909), cols. 104–106.

41   *Ibid.*

42   See p. 26.

43   For example, see pp. 19, 20.

44   See, for example, M.E. Alflatt, "The Responsibility for Involuntary Sin in Saint Augustine," in *Recherches augustiniennes* 10 (Paris: Études Augustiniennes, 1975), 179.

45   Another place Augustine accuses the Manichees of concupiscence is in *Gen. Man.* II.xxvi.39.

46   Augustine's reference to the "root" may have Manichaean overtones, for the term is a technical expression in many Manichaean texts outside African Manichaeism. Fortunatus uses the parable of two kinds of trees generating from two different "roots" to support his argument for dualism (*Fort.* 22). See Decret, *Aspects du Manichéisme*, 196.

47   See p. 55.

48   A prior allusion to this verse has already been made in *Gen. Man.* I.xxiii.40.

49   Babcock, "Sin and Moral Agency," 30–31.

Chapter Five

1   E.g., J. Rist, "Augustine on Free Will and Predestination," *Journal of Theological Studies* N.S. 20 (1969): 420–447.

2   *Conf.* XIII.xxxv.50 (CC, 27/1, 272 = PL, 32, col. 867): "Domine deus, pacem da nobis—omnia enim praestitisti nobis—pacem quietis, pacem sabbati, pacem sine uespera. Omnis quippe iste ordo pulcherrimus rerum ualde bonarum modis suis peractis transiturus est: et mane quippe in eis factum est et uespera."

3   E. Buonaiuti argues that even Augustine's use of the term *massa* is not without Manichaean influence. Consequently, Augustine might have interpreted Paul's metaphor of the potter and clay as an absolute statement of human destiny. See E. Buonaiuti, "Manichaeism and Augustine's Idea of 'Massa Perditionis'," *Harvard Theological Review* 20 (1927): 123–124.

4   *Mor.* II.vi.8 (CSEL, 90, 94–95 = PL, 32, col. 1348): "Haec uero quae tendunt esse,
     ad ordinem tendunt; quem cum fuerint consecuta, ipsum esse consequuntur,
     quantum id creatura consequi potest. Ordo enim ad conuenientiam quandam quod
     ordinat redigit. Nihil est autem esse, quam unum esse. Itaque in quantum quidque
     unitatem adipiscitur, in tantum est. Unitatis est enim operatio, conuenientia et
     concordia, qua sunt in quantum sunt ea quae composita sunt, nam simplicia per se
     sunt, quia una sunt; quae autem non sunt simplicia, concordia partium imitantur
     unitatem et in tantum sunt in quantum assequuntur. Quare ordinatio esse cogit,
     inordinatio ergo non esse; quae peruersio etiam nominatur atque corruptio."

5   *Mor.* II.vii.9 (CSEL, 90, 95 = PL, 32, col. 1349): "Sed dei bonitas eo rem perduci
     non sinit et omnia deficientia sic ordinat, ut ibi sint ubi congruentissime possint
     esse, donec ordinatis motibus ad id recurrant unde defecerunt. Itaque etiam animas
     rationales, in quibus potentissimum est liberum arbitrium, deficientes a se in
     inferioribus creaturae gradibus ordinat, ubi esse tales decet. Fiunt ergo miseriae
     diuino iudicio, dum conuenienter pro meritis ordinantur."

6   On Augustine's concept of order, see T.A. Lacey, *Nature, Miracle and Sin: A Study
     of St. Augustine's Conception of Natural Order,* The Pringle Stuart Lectures for
     1914 (London: Longmans, Green, 1916), 92–114; see also B.T. McDonough, "The
     Notion of Order in St. Augustine's 'On Free Choice of the Will'," *Irish
     Theological Quarterly* 46 (1979): 51–55.

7   *Mor.* II.vii.10 (CSEL, 90, 96 = PL, 32, col. 1349): "Satis est [...] ut uideatis nullum
     esse de bono et malo religiosae disputationis exitum, nisi quicquid est, in quantum
     est, ex deo sit, in quantum autem ab essentia deficit, non sit ex deo, sed tamen
     diuina prouidentia semper, sicut uniuersitati congruit, ordinetur."

8   Our reconstruction of Augustine's understanding of the cosmogonic myth is
     indebted to Coyle's synthesis which makes special reference to the Augustinian
     sources (*Augustine's "De Moribus"*, 30–50), and to Decret's account of the North
     African Manichaean teachings (*Aspects du Manichéisme*, 193–322).

9   See chapter 1, n. 44.

10   Cf. N.J. Torchia, "The Significance of *Ordo* in St. Augustine's Moral Theory," in
     Collectanea Augustiniana: Augustine, Presbyter Factus Sum, papers originally
     presented at a conference at Marquette University, Nov. 1990, eds. J.T. Lienhard,
     E.C. Muller & R.J. Teske, (New York: Peter Lang, 1993), 264–267.

11   Doignon seems to make a similar distinction between the ontological and
     epistemological questions when he addresses the problems of nature and art. J.
     Doignon, "Le *De ordine,* son déroulement, ses thèmes," in *L'opera letteraria di
     Agostino tra Cassiciacum e Milano,* Agostino nelle terre di Ambrogio (1–4 ottobre
     1986), eds. G. Reale, et al. (Palermo: Edizioni Augustinus, 1987), 148.

12   See Plotinus' *Enn.* III.ii.17; I.vi.2. The moral emphasis of the issue is due to
     Ciceronian influence. See J. Doignon, "Le *De ordine,*" 121, and A. Solignac,
     "Réminiscences plotiniennes et porphyriennes dans le début du *De ordine* de saint
     Augustin," *Archives de philosophie* 20 (1957): 454. Cf. J. Rief, *Der Ordobegriff
     des jungen Augustinus,* (Abhandlungen zur Moraltheologie, 2) (Paderborn: F.
     Schöningh, 1962), 73–80.

13 J. McWilliam, "The Cassiciacum Autobiography," in *Studia Patristica* 18/4, papers presented to the Ninth International Conference on Patristic Studies held in Oxford 1983, ed. E.A. Livingstone (Leuven: Peeters Press, 1990), 20, 40.

14 *Ord.* II.iv.11 (CC, 29, 113 = PL, 32, col. 1000): "Non enim illa commemoratio tenebrarum ad id, quod a me inuolutum prolatum erat, parum nobis attulit luminis. Namque omnis uita stultorum quamuis per eos ipsos minime constans minimeque ordinata sit, per diuinam tamen prouidentiam necessario rerum ordine includitur et quasi quibusdam locis illa ineffabili et sempiterna lege dispositis nullo modo esse sinitur, ubi esse non debet. Ita fit, ut angusto animo ipsam solam quisque considerans ueluti magna repercussus foeditate auersetur. Si autem mentis oculos erigens atque diffundens simul uniuersa conlustret, nihil non ordinatum suisque semper ueluti sedibus distinctum dispositumque reperiet."

15 It is clear that Augustine equates moral disorder with moral evil in his illustrations (*ord.* II.iv.12). The ensuing question is equivalent to asking whether evil originates from God or apart from God who orders everything (II.vii.23). The concern about the origin of evil certainly has a Manichaean ring to it (Doignon, "Le *De ordine*," 149). Augustine, however, will leave the question open until he writes *De libero arbitrio*. For now, he is satisfied with Monica's answer which he summarizes in a statement: "tamen etiam ista omnia, quae fatemur esse peruersa, non esse praeter diuinum ordinem" (*ord.* II.vii.24: CC, 29, 120 = PL, 32, col. 1006).

16 Hence, Augustine mentions the analogical notion of "darkness" in the beginning of the cited passage (cf. *ord.* II.iii.10).

17 Augustine uses these two terms (in adverbial form) as synonyms in *ord.* II.viii.25 and II.xix.49.

18 In the Plotinian context, God is the highest and truest unity. Cf. U.G. Leinsle, "Von der Weltordnung zur Lebensordnung: Aufgabe und Grenze der Philosophie nach Augustinus' Dialog *De Ordine*," *Theologisch-praktische Quartalschrift* 137 (1989): 377.

19 Doignon suggests that the liberal arts disciplines treated by Augustine were considered encyclopedic during the imperial period. Thus, Augustine might have deemed that, having seen a unifying order in all the divergent branches of learning, one's rational vision is well adjusted to contemplate the divine. Doignon, "Le *De ordine*," 143–145.

20 *Uer. rel.* xxvii.50 (CC, 32, 219–220 = PL, 34, col. 144): "Sicut autem isti ambo nullo dubitante ita sunt, ut unum eorum, id est ueterem atque terrenum possit in hac tota uita unus homo agere, nouum uero et caelestem nemo in hac uita possit nisi cum uetere, nam et ab ipso incipiat necesse est et usque ad uisibilem mortem cum illo quamuis eo deficiente se proficiente perduret, sic proportione uniuersum genus humanum, cuius tamquam unius hominis uita est ab Adam usque ad finem huius saeculi, ita sub diuinae prouidentiae legibus administratur, ut in duo genera distributum appareat. Quorum in uno est turba impiorum terreni hominis imaginem ab initio saeculi usque ad finem gerentium, in altero series populi uni deo dediti [...]. Resurget ergo pius populus, ut ueteris hominis sui reliquias transformet in nouum. Resurget autem impius populus, qui ab initio usque ad finem ueterem hominem gessit, ut in secundam mortem praecipitetur."

21   Cf. K.A. Wohlfarth, *Der metaphysische Ansatz bei Augustinus*, (Monographien zur philosophischen Forschung, 60) (Meisenheim am Glan: Anton Hain, 1969), 67–76.

22   F. De Capitani traces Augustine's use of *corruptio* in the anti-Manichaean writings and concludes that the term is progressively equated with *malum*. It indicates Augustine's inability to distance himself from the Manichaean line of questioning on the issue of evil. See F. De Capitani, "*Corruptio* negli scritti antimanichei di S. Agostino: Il fenomeno e la natura della corruzione," *Rivista di Filosofia neo-scolastica* 72 (1980): 644.

23   See p. 56.

24   Cf. R.J. O'Connell, "*De libero arbitrio* I: Stoicism Revisited," *Augustinian Studies* 1 (1970): 66, 68.

25   Cf. G. Madec, "Vnde malum? Le livre I du *de libero arbitrio*," in "*De Libero Arbitrio*" *di Agostino d'Ippona*, commented by G. Madec, et al., (Lectio Augustini, 6) (Palermo: Ed. Augustinus, 1990), 32; O'Connell, "Stoicism Revisited," 58–63.

26   This may indicate that Augustine did in his early days hold to the view of man as "fallen souls," which R.J. O'Connell has contended for many years. See R.J. Teske, "St. Augustine's View of the Original Human Condition in *De Genesi contra Manichaeos*," *Augustinian Studies* 22 (1991): 141–155, and R.J. O'Connell, "The 'De Genesi contra Manichaeos' and the Origin of the Soul," *Revue des études augustiniennes* 39 (1993): 129–141.

27   Van Fleteren, "Augustine's *De vera religione*," 475–477.

28   *Uer. rel.* xii.24 (CC, 32, 202 = PL, 34, col. 132): "Si autem dum in hoc stadio uitae humanae anima degit, uincat eas, quas aduersum se nutriuit, cupiditates fruendo mortalibus et ad eas uincendas gratia dei se adiuuari credat, mente illi seruiens et bona uoluntate; sine dubitatione reparabitur, et a multis mutabilibus ad unum incommutabile reuertetur [...]." (see also xv.29.)

29   Van Fleteren similarly observes that although Augustine still shows confidence in human ability to attain to the vision of God, he begins to see one's need of divine help in doing so ("Augustine's *De vera religione*," 481–482).

30   N.W. Den Bok, "Freedom of the Will: A Systematic and Biographical Sounding of Augustine's Thoughts on Human Willing," *Augustiniana* 44 (1994): 256, 269–270.

31   The term "tripartite" should not be taken too literally in describing Augustine's anthropology. See J. Rivière, trans., "*De fide et symbolo*," in *Oeuvres de saint Augustin*, vol. 9: *Exposés généraux de la foi: De fide et symbolo, Enchiridion*, 2nd ed., (Bibliothèque augustinienne, 1re série: Opuscules) (Paris: Études Augustiniennes, 1988), 66, n. 1.

32   *Fid. sym.* x.23 (CSEL, 41, 29 = PL, 40, col. 194): "Sed non tam cito anima subiugatur spiritui ad bonam operationem, quam cito spiritus deo ad uerum fidem et bonam uoluntatem, sed aliquando tardius eius inpetus, quo in carnalia et temporalia diffluit, refrenatur. Sed quoniam et ipsa mundatur, recipiens stabilitatem naturae suae dominate spiritu [...]."

33   Cf. Prendiville, "Development of the Idea of Habit," 71.

34 See also *ibid.*, 72.

35 See B. De Margerie, *Introduction à l'histoire de l'exégèse*, vol. 3: *Saint Augustin* (Paris: Les Éditions du Cerf, 1983), 142.

36 Cf. *idem*, "*Praeparatio Cordis ad Plura Perferenda*: S. Augustin, *De Sermone Domini in Monte* I,19,59 et 20,66 (Mt 5,39ss)," *Augustinianum* 32 (1992): 157.

37 *Ser. dom.* I.xxiii.78 (CC, 35, 87–88 = PL, 34, col. 1268): "[...] nos autem potestate accepta efficimur filii, in quantum ea quae ab illo praecipiuntur implemus. [...] Itaque non ait: Facite ista, quia estis filii, sed: Facite ista, ut sitis filii."

38 Fredriksen, "Early Interpretation," 121–128; cf. A. Pincherle, "Romani 5, 12–13 in s. Agostino," *Studi e materiali di storia delle religioni* 37 (1966): 280.

39 W.S. Babcock, "Augustine's Interpretation of Romans (A.D. 394–396)," *Augustinian Studies* 10 (1979): 61. A similar observation is made by Prendiville concerning *Expositio epistulae ad Galatas* ("Development of the Idea of Habit," 75).

40 *Exp. Rom.* 38:46 (CSEL, 84, 20 = PL, 35, col. 2072): "Legem autem peccati dicit ex transgressione Adae conditionem mortalem, qua mortales facti sumus. Ex hac enim labe carnis concupiscentia carnalis sollicitat [...]."

41 *Exp. Rom.* 47:55 (CSEL, 84, 30 = PL, 35, col. 2076): "Quoniam quos ante praesciuit, et praedestinauit conformes imaginis filii eius."

42 *Exp. Rom.* 47:55 (CSEL, 84, 30 = PL, 35, cols. 2076–2077): "Non enim omnes, qui uocati sunt, secundum propositum uocati sunt, hoc enim propositum ad praescientiam et ad praedestinationem dei pertinet. Nec praedestinavit aliquem, nisi quem praescivit crediturum et secuturum uocationem suam, quos et electos dicit. Multi enim non ueniunt, cum uocati fuerint, nemo autem uenit, qui uocatus non fuerit."

43 *Exp. Rom.* 52:60 (CSEL, 84, 34 = PL, 35, cols. 2078–2079): "[...] aequales enim omnes sunt ante meritum nec potest in rebus omnino aequalibus electio nominari."

44 *Exp. Rom.* 52:60 (CSEL, 84, 35 = PL, 35, col. 2079): "Est autem gratia, ut uocatio peccatori praerogatur, cum eius merita nulla, nisi ad damnationem praecesserint. Quod si uocatus uocantem secutus fuerit, quod est iam in libero arbitrio, merebitur et spiritum sanctum per quem bona possit operari, in quo permanens—quod nihilominus est in libero arbitrio—merebitur etiam uitam aeternam, quae nulla possit labe corrumpi."

45 Cf. A.F.N. Lekkerkerker, *Römer 7 und Römer 9 bei Augustin* (Amsterdam: H.J. Paris, 1942), 99–100; M. Löhrer, *Der Glaubensbegriff des hl. Augustinus in seinen ersten Schriften bis zu den Confessiones* (Einsiedeln: Benziger Verlag, 1955), 247–248; G. Hultgren, *Le commandement d'amour chez Augustin: interprétation philosophique et théologique d'après les écrits de la période 386–400* (Paris: Vrin, 1939), 93.

46 Augustine later touches on the idea of "hiddenness" in his quotation of Dt. 29:29: "Quae occulta sunt deo, quae autem palam sunt, uobis et filiis uestris" (*exp. Rom.* 71:79: CSEL, 84, 49 = PL, 35, col. 2086).

47 Almut Mutzenbecher suggests that the timeframe of the composition of the whole
    of *De sermone domini in monte* to be between the end of 392 and the end of 396
    (*Sancti Aurelii Augustini De Sermone Domini in Monte libros duos*, [Corpus
    Christianum, 35] [Turnholti: Brepols, 1967], ix). However, Denis Joseph
    Kavanagh argues that the work is probably an elaboration of earlier sermons in the
    cathedral of Hippo in view of the fact that Augustine resolved not to deal with
    difficult questions in oral discourses. D.J. Kavanagh, trans., *St. Augustine:
    Commentary on the Lord's Sermon on the Mount: With Seventeen Related
    Sermons*, (The Fathers of the Church, 11) (New York: CIMA, 1951), 3. If that is
    so, Augustine must have been systematically preaching on the Matthaean text of
    the Sermon on the Mount some time in the first half of 395 before he wrote to
    Alypius, the bishop of Thagaste, a little after May 4 (Perler, *Voyages*, 436–437),
    reporting the incidents on the feast of the Laetitia (*epis.* XXIX). The day the
    incidents occurred, Augustine preached on Mt. 7:6, and only a few days later was
    he preaching on Mt. 7:16 (XXIX.2 & 6). The ideas in the exposition of Mt. 7:6 as
    shown in the letter indicate agreement with Augustine's treatment of the same text
    in *ser. dom.* II.xx.68. Furthermore, Augustine in his letter to Paulinus around this
    time (mid-April/mid-May of 395; Perler, *Voyages*, 436–437) praised the latter for
    having *simplicitas cordis*—the main theme of *De sermone domini in monte* II
    (*epis.* XXVII). (Incidentally, this could well be the only letter in this early period
    that contains the term *simplicitas cordis*, found in only two other letters: *epis.*
    CXLVII [413] & CCXLIII [unknown date]). This may suggest Augustine's
    dominating concern around this time, in which case he might have worked on his
    exposition not too long after the delivery of his sermons. All these indicators
    suggest that Book Two of *De sermone domini in monte* was composed between
    April and June of 395, right before his ordination as bishop (which took place
    between mid-May and mid-June of 395, according to Perler, *Voyages*, 436–437).
    Accordingly, Book Two would represent a view beyond that expressed in
    Augustine's three treatises on Romans and Galatians, but prior to his shift in *Ad
    Simplicianum*.

48 *Ser. dom.* II.vi.21 (CC, 35, 111 = PL, 34, col. 1278): "[...] cum praecesserit bona
    uoluntas nostra, quae uocantem sequitur, perficiatur in nobis uoluntas dei [...]."

49 In *exp. Rom.* 54:62, Augustine did mention that divine judgment of election is
    hidden to earthly persons; but at least it is open to the spiritual.

50 The concept of *ordo occultus* appeared as early as *Acad.* I.i.1 to explain the
    common idea of fortune. In other places, it is assumed to be operating without
    human awareness (*ord.* I.xi.33; II.xx.54; *Adim.* xvii.3; *epis.* XXIX.2). But *occultus
    poenarum ordo* is used in *Faus.* XXII.78 in the context of predestination.

51 See p. 77.

52 Rondet also seems to consider *quest.* 68 as the last stage of Augustine's
    development just before the writing of *Ad Simplicianum* ("La prédestination
    augustinienne," 232, esp. n. 20). Other than the appearance of more developed
    ideas concerning election, there are two important citations from the Matthaean
    text of the Sermon on the Mount. The first is from Mt. 7:6 on not giving holy
    things to dogs and pearls to swine. The second is from Mt. 5:8 on purity of the
    heart. The latter is accompanied by another citation of Wis. 1:1 which explicitly
    mentions *simplicitas cordis*.

53 Subtle differences also occur in the usage of terminology. Fredriksen, "Early Interpretation," 136–138; A. Vanneste, "Saint Paul et la doctrine augustinienne du péché originel," in *Studiorum Paulinorum, Congressus Internationalis Catholicus, 1961, Romae*, vol. 2, (Analecta Biblica, 18) (Romae: E Pontificio Instituto Biblico, 1963), 514–515.

54 Cf. G. Martinetto, "Les premières réactions augustiniennes de Pélage," *Revue des études augustiniennes* 17 (1971): 104–105.

55 *Diu. quaes.*, quest. 68, 5 (CC, 44a, 181 = PL, 40, col. 73): "Et quoniam nec uelle quisquam potest nisi admonitus et uocatus, siue intrinsecus ubi nullus hominum uidet, siue extrinsecus per sermonem sonantem aut aliqua signa uisibilia, efficitur ut etiam ipsum uelle deus operetur in nobis."

56 *Diu. quaes.*, quest. 68, 5 (CC, 44a, 180 = PL, 40, col. 73): "[...] non uolentis neque currentis, sed miserentis est dei [...]."

57 Scholars have traditionally argued that *Ad Simplicianum* marks the beginning of Augustine's mature view. E.g., Portalié, "Augustin (saint)," col. 2379; Rondet, "La prédestination augustinienne: Genèse d'une doctrine," *Sciences ecclésiastiques* 18 (1966): 233; D. Marafioti, "Alle origini del teorema della predestinazione (Simpl. I, 2, 13–22)," in *Congresso internazionale su s. Agostino nel XVI centenario della conversione*, Roma 15–20 settembre 1986, vol. 2, (Studia Ephemeridis Augustinianum, 25) (Roma: Institutum Patristicum Augustinianum, 1987), 257–277. For a recent defence of the traditional view, see P. Rigby, *Original Sin in Augustine's "Confessions"* (Ottawa: University of Ottawa Press, 1987), 19.

58 Fredriksen, "Early Interpretation," 192–194; cf. H. Jonas, *Augustin und das paulinische Freiheitsproblem: Eine philosophische Studie zum pelagianischen Streit* (Forschungen zur Religion und Literatur des Alten und Neuen Testaments, Neue Folge, Heft 27. Der ganzen Reihe, Heft 44) (Göttingen: Vandenhoeck & Ruprecht, 1965), 41; Lekkerkerker, *Römer 7 und Römer 9*, 129.

59 This is the first occurrence of the term *peccatum originale*.

60 *Simpl.* I.ii.10 (CC, 44, 35 = PL, 40, col. 117): "Aliter enim deus praestat ut uelimus, aliter praestat quod uoluerimus. Ut uelimus enim et suum esse uoluit et nostrum, suum uocando nostrum sequendo. Quod autem uoluerimus solus praestat, id est posse bene agere et semper beate uiuere." Cf. A. Pincherle, *La formazione theologica di sant' Agostino* (Roma: Edizioni italiane, 1947), 153.

61 In regard to the development of Augustine's understanding of the will in this early mature period, see Judith Chelius Stark's analysis of the theme in *conf.* VIII. J.C. Stark, "The Pauline Influence on Augustine's Notion of the Will," *Vigiliae Christianae* 43 (1989), 345–361.

62 *Simpl.* I.ii.22 (CC, 44, 55 = PL, 40, col. 128): "Sed uoluntas ipsa, nisi aliquid occurrerit quod delectet atque inuitet animum, moueri nullo modo potest." For the role of "delight," see Brown, *Augustine of Hippo*, 154–155.

63 *Simpl.* I.ii.22 (CC, 44, 56 = PL, 40, col. 128): "Credamus tantum, et si capere non ualemus, quoniam qui uniuersam creaturam et spiritualem et corporalem fecit et condidit, omnia in numero et pondere et mensura disponit. Sed inscrutabilia sunt iudicia eius, et inuestigabiles uiae eius."

64   *Faus.* XXII.78 (CSEL, 25/1, 679 = PL, 42, col. 451): "Sed quae sit distributio
      iudicantis et miserantis dei, cur alius sic, alius autem sic, occultis fit causis, iustis
      tamen. Non tamen ideo nescimus omnia ista iudicio aut misericordia dei fieri, licet
      in abdito positis mensuris et numeris et ponderibus, quibus omnia disponuntur a
      deo creatore omnium, quae naturaliter sunt [...]."

65   This view of Augustine has come a long way when compared with his early
      angeology (around 388) which considers that angels are "not higher than Man's
      mens when it adheres to God" (Coyle, *Augustine's "De Moribus"*, 338).

66   See J.J. O'Donnell, *Augustine: Confessions*, vol. 3: *Commentary on Books 8–13,
      Indexes* (Oxford: Clarendon Press, 1992), 414.

67   *Conf.* XIII.xxxiv.49 (CC, 27, 271 = PL, 32, col. 866): "Inspeximus etiam, propter
      quorum figurationem ista uel tali ordine fieri uel tali ordine scribi uoluisti, et
      uidemus, quia bona sunt singula et omnia bona ualde, in uerbo tuo, in unico tuo,
      caelum et terram, caput et corpus ecclesiae, in praedestinatione ante omnia tempora
      sine mane et uespera."

Conclusion

1   Pelikan, *The Christian Tradition*, vol. 1, 280.   Although Pelikan admits that
     Augustine drew on both Ambrose's notion of sinless conception of Christ and
     Cyprian's view of infant baptism to formulate the doctrine of original sin, he also
     seems to recognize that the two Christian writers did not exploit the implied
     determinism in their ideas (*ibid.*, 290–291). Therefore, the question remains: What
     could have triggered Augustine into exploiting that implication?

2   See Ambrose, *De Cain et Abel* I.i.4.   Joanne McWilliam argues that Augustine
     possibly drew on Ambrose's discussion of Esau and Jacob in *De fuga saeculi*
     viii.48–50 for idea of congruent grace.   See J. McWilliam, "Augustine and
     Ambrose's *sanam fidem*," in *Charisteria Augustiniana: Josepho Oroz Reta Dicata*,
     eds. P. Merino & J.M. Torrecilla, (*Augustinus* 38) (Madrid: Ed. Augustinus, 1993),
     347–357.   Nevertheless, that reference to Ambrose's special understanding of grace
     remains an isolated incidence and only occurs in the allegorical context of the
     search for God's word, not of salvation.

3   E.g., see Ambrose, *Explanatio psalmorum xii* XXXVII.viii.3, XLVII.vii.3;
     Expositio psalmi cxviii VIII.34, XIII.27.

4   Fortunatus and Faustus as well as Felix, all affirm that sinning is involuntary. (See
     Decret, *Aspects du Manichéisme*, 272, 278, 290.) Felix considers it unthinkable if,
     given a choice, one does not choose what is good. To sin by free will is impossible
     (*Fel.* II.viii).

5   C.J. Brunner similarly noted Augustine's dilemma, that he is unable to escape from
     his own version of determinism after trying to flee from that in Manichaeism. See
     C.J. Brunner, "The Ontological Relation Between Evil and Existents in
     Manichaean Texts and in Augustine's Interpretation of Manichaeism," in
     Philosophies of Existence, Ancient and Medieval, ed. P. Morewedge (New York:
     Fordham University Press, 1982), 78–95.

6   Why God in his power does not elect all to be saved? Augustine's resort to divine
     mystery does not squarely confront the issue of God's love. T.T. Shimmyo suggests
     a version of limited predestination: God in his love predestines all to be saved, but
     his purpose could be frustrated by factors other than God's will, such as a lack of
     human response. See T.T. Shimmyo, "Free Will in St. Augustine's Doctrine of
     Predestination," *Patristic and Byzantine Review* 6 (1987): 136–145.

BIBLIOGRAPHY

Alfaric, Prosper. *L'évolution intellectuelle de saint Augustin*. Paris: E. Nourry, 1918.

Alflatt, Malcolm E. "The Responsibility for Involuntary Sin in Saint Augustine." In *Recherches augustiniennes* 10. Paris: Études Augustiniennes, 1975, 171–186.

Allberry, C.R.C., ed. *A Manichaean Psalm-Book*. Part II. With a contribution by H. Ibscher. (Manichaean Manuscripts in the Chester Beatty Collection, 2). Stuttgart: W. Kohlhammer, 1938.

Augustine on Human Goodness: Metaphysics, Ethics and Politics. Proceedings of the 21st Annual Philosophy Colloquium, Dayton, Apr. 7–9, 1994. Directed by R. Herbenick & P.A. Johnson. Published in *University of Dayton Review* 22 (1994).

Babcock, William S. "Augustine on Sin and Moral Agency." *Journal of Religious Ethics* 16 (1988): 28–55.

———. "Augustine's Interpretation of Romans (A.D. 394–396)." *Augustinian Studies* 10 (1979): 55–74.

Barbone, Steven. "*Frugalitas* in Saint Augustine." *Augustiniana* 44 (1994): 5–15.

BeDuhn, Jason David. "A Regimen for Salvation: Medical Models in Manichaean Asceticism." *Semeia* 58 (1992): 109–134.

Berthold, Fred. "Free Will and Theodicy in Augustine: An Exposition and Critique." *Religious Studies* 17 (1981): 525–535.

Bianchi, Ugo. "Sur la question des deux âmes de l'homme dans le manichéisme." In *A Green Leaf.* Papers in honour of Professor Jes P. Asmussen. Edited by J. Duchesne-Guillemin. (Acta Iranica, 28; Hommages et Opera Minora, 12). Leiden: E.J. Brill, 1988, 311–316.

Bonner, Gerald. *St. Augustine of Hippo: Life and Controversies.* Revised ed. Norwich: The Canterbury Press, 1986.

Brown, Peter. *Augustine of Hippo: A Biography.* Berkeley: University of California Press, 1967.

Brunner, Christopher J. "The Ontological Relation Between Evil and Existents in Manichaean Texts and in Augustine's Interpretation of Manichaeism." In *Philosophies of Existence, Ancient and Midieval.* Edited by P. Morewedge. New York: Fordham University Press, 1982, 78–95.

Buonaiuti, E. "Manichaeism and Augustine's Idea of *Massa Perditionis.*" *Harvard Theological Review* 20 (1927): 117–127.

Burleigh, John H.S., ed. *Augustine: Earlier Writings.* (The Library of Christian Classics, 6). London: SCM Press, 1953.

Burns, J. Patout. *The Development of Augustine's Doctrine of Operative Grace.* Paris: Études Augustiniennes, 1980.

Chapman, Emmanuel. *Saint Augustine's Philosophy of Beauty.* (Saint Michael's Mediaeval Studies. Monograph series). New York: Sheed & Ward, 1939.

Cooper, Robert M. "Saint Augustine's Doctrine of Evil." *Scottish Journal of Theology* 16 (1963): 256–276.

Courcelle, Pierre. *Recherches sur les Confessions de saint Augustin.* Revised ed. Paris: Éditions E. de Boccard, 1968.

Coyle, J. Kevin. *Augustine's "De Moribus Ecclesiae Catholicae": A Study of the Work, its Composition and its Sources.* (Paradosis, 25). Fribourg: University Press, 1978.

———. "The Idea of the 'Good' in Manichaeism." Forthcoming in *Proceedings of the Fourth International Conference on Manichaeism.* Berlin, July 14–18, 1997. Edited by W. Sundermann. Berlin: Claudius Naumann, 124–137.

Cress, Donald A. "Hierius & St. Augustine's Account of the Lost *De Pulchro et Apto*: *Confessions* IV, 13–15." *Augustinian Studies* 7 (1976): 153–163.

De Capitani, Franco. "*Corruptio* negli scritti antimanichei di S. Agostino: Il fenomeno e la natura della corruzione." *Rivista di Filosofia neo-scolastica* 72 (1980): 640–669.

De Margerie, Bertrand. *Introduction à l'histoire de l'exégèse*, vol. 3: *Saint Augustin*. Paris: Les Éditions du Cerf, 1983.

———. "*Praeparatio Cordis ad Plura Perferenda*: S. Augustin, *De Sermone Domini in Monte* I,19,59 et 20,66 (Mt 5,39ss)." *Augustinianum* 32 (1992): 145–160.

Decret, François. *L'Afrique manichéenne, IVe – Ve siècles: Étude historique et doctrinale.* 2 vols. Paris: Études Augustiniennes, 1978.

———. *Aspects du Manichéisme dans l'Afrique romaine: Les controverses de Fortunatus, Faustus et Félix avec saint Augustin.* Paris: Études Augustiniennes, 1970.

———. "Le *Globus horribilis* dans l'eschatologie manichéenne d'après les traités de saint Augustin." In *Mélanges d'histoire des religions offerts à Henri-Charles Puech.* Sous le patronage et avec le concours du Collège de France et de la Section des sciences religieuses de l'Ecole pratique des hautes études. Paris: Presses Universitaires de France, 1974, 487–492.

———. "Le manichéisme présentait-il en Afrique et à Rome des particularismes régionaux distinctifs?" *Augustinianum* 34 (1994), 5–40.

Den Bok, Nico W. "Freedom of the Will: A Systematic and Biographical Sounding of Augustine's Thoughts on Human Willing." *Augustiniana* 44 (1994): 237–270.

Doignon, Jean. "Augustin, *De beata vita* 4,34: *Sapientia dei* est-elle une appellation impersonnelle?" In *De Tertullien aux Mozarabes: Antiquité tardive et christianisme ancien (IIIe–VIe siècles): Mélanges offerts à Jacques Fontaine.* Edited by L. Holtz & J.-C. Fredouille. Paris: Études augustinniennes, 1992, 151–155.

———. "Le *De ordine*, son déroulement, ses thèmes." In *L'opera letteraria di Agostino tra Cassiciacum e Milano.* Agostino nelle terre di Ambrogio (1–4 ottobre 1986). Edited by G. Reale, et al. Palermo: Edizioni Augustinus, 1987, 113–150.

———. "Notes complémentaires." In *Oeuvres de saint Augustin.* Vol. 4/1: *Dialogues philosophiques: De beata vita—La vie heureuse.* Revised ed. (Bibliothèque augustinienne, 1re série: Opuscules). Paris: Desclée de Brouwer, 1986, 133–152.

———. "Souvenirs cicéroniens (Hortensius, Consolation) et virgiliens dans l'exposé d'Augustin sur l'état humain d''ignorance et de difficulté' (Aug., lib. arb. 3, 51–54)." *Vigiliae Christianae* 47 (1993): 131–139.

Du Roy, Olivier. *L'intelligence de la foi en la Trinité selon saint Augustin: Genèse de sa théologie trinitaire jusqu'en 391.* Paris: Études Augustiniennes, 1966.

Eborowicz, W. *La contemplation selon Plotin.* (Biblioteca del 'Giornale di metafisica,' 14). Torino: Societa Editrice Internazionale, 1958.

Eliade, Mircea, et al., eds., *The Encyclopedia of Religion*, vol. 6. New York: MacMillan, 1987. S.v. "Good, The," by L. Kolakowski.

Eschweiler, Karl. *Die ästhetischen Elemente in der Religionsphilosophie des hl. Augustin.* Inaugural-Dissertation der philosophischen Fakultät (Sektion I) an der Ludwig-Maximilians-Universität München zur Erlangung der Doktorwürde am 11. Juni

1909 vorgelegt. Euskirchen: Buchdruckerei der Euskirchener Volkszeitung, 1909.

Evans, Gillian R. *Augustine on Evil*. Cambridge: Cambridge University Press, 1982; reprint, 1991.

Feldmann, Erich. *Die "Epistola Fundamenti" der nordafrikanischen Manichäer: Versuch einer Rekonstruktion*. Altenberge: Akademische Bibliothek, 1987.

Ferrari, Leo Charles. "Astronomy and Augustine's Break with the Manichees." *Revue d'études augustiniennes* 19 (1973): 263–276.

————. "Augustine and Astrology." *Laval théologique et philosophique* 33 (1977): 241–251.

————. "Augustine's 'Nine Years' as a Manichee." *Augustiniana* 25 (1975): 210–216.

————. "Young Augustine: Both Catholic and Manichee." *Augustinian Studies* 26 (1995): 109–128.

Ferwerda, R. "Two Souls: Origen's and Augustine's Attitude Toward the Two Souls Doctrine, its Place in Greek and Christian Philosophy." *Vigiliae Christianae* 37 (1983): 360–378.

Fontanier, Jean-Michel. "Sur le traité d'Augustin *De pulchro et apto*: Convenance, beauté et adaptation." *Revue des sciences philosophiques et théologiques* 73 (1989): 413–421.

Fredriksen, Paula Lee. "Augustine's Early Interpretation of Paul." Ph.D. diss., Princeton University, 1979.

Frend, W.H.C. "The Gnostic-Manichaean Tradition in Roman North Africa." *Journal of Ecclesiastical History* 4 (1953): 13–26.

Grondijs, L.H. "Analyse du Manichéisme Numidien au IVe siècle." In *Augustinus Magister*. Congrès international augustinien, Paris, 21–24 septembre 1954, vol. 3. Paris: Études Augustiniennes, 1954–1955, 391–410.

Bibliography

———. "Numidian Manicheism in Augustinus Time." *Nederlands Theologisch Tijdschrift* 9 (1954): 21–42.

Harrison, Carol. *Beauty and Revelation in the Thought of Saint Augustine.* Oxford: Clarendon Press, 1992.

———. "Measure, Number and Weight in Saint Augustine's Aesthetics." *Augustinianum* 28 (1988): 591–602.

Hastings, James, ed., *Encyclopaedia of Religion and Ethics*, vol. 6. Edinburgh: T. & T. Clark, 1914. S.v. "Goodness," by J. Strahan.

Hohensee, H. *The Augustinian Concept of Authority.* (*Folia*, Supplement II). New York: Paulist Press, 1954.

Hultgren, Gunnar. *Le commandement d'amour chez Augustin: interprétation philosophique et théologique d'après les écrits de la période 386–400.* Paris: Vrin, 1939.

Jonas, Hans. *Augustin und das paulinische Freiheitsproblem: Eine philosophische Studie zum pelagianischen Streit.* (Forschungen zur Religion und Literatur des Alten und Neuen Testaments, Neue Folge, Heft 27. Der ganzen Reihe, Heft 44). Göttingen: Vandenhoeck & Ruprecht, 1965.

Katô, Takeshi. "*Melodia interior*: sur le traité *De pulchro et apto*." *Revue des études augustiniennes* 12 (1966): 229–240.

Kavanagh, Denis Joseph, trans. *St. Augustine: Commentary on the Lord's Sermon on the Mount: With Seventeen Related Sermons.* (The Fathers of the Church, 11). New York: CIMA, 1951.

Kikushi, S. "On Augustine's Understanding of the Created Good." *Studies in Medieval Thought* 31 (1989): 76–83.

Kreuzer, Johann. *Pulchritudo: Vom Erkennen Gottes bei Augustin Bemerkungen zu den Büchern IX, X und XI der 'Confessiones'.* München: Wilhelm Fink Verlag, 1995.

Lacey, Thomas Alexander. *Nature, Miracle and Sin: A Study of St. Augustine's Conception of Natural Order.* The Pringle Stuart Lectures for 1914. London: Longmans, Green, 1916, 92–114.

Leinsle, Ulrich G. "Von der Weltordnung zur Lebensordnung: Aufgabe und Grenze der Philosophie nach Augustinus' Dialog *De Ordine.*" *Theologisch-praktische Quartalschrift* 137 (1989): 369–377.

Lekkerkerker, Arie F.N. *Römer 7 und Römer 9 bei Augustin.* Amsterdam: H.J. Paris, 1942.

Lieu, Judith M. & Samuel N.C. Lieu, "*Felix Conversus ex Manichaeis*: A Case of Mistaken Identity." *Journal of Theological Studies* 32 (1981): 173–176. Reprinted in Lieu, Samuel N.C. *Manichaeism in Mesopotamia and the Roman East.* (Religions in the Graeco-Roman World, 118). Leiden: E.J. Brill, 1994, 153–155.

Lieu, Samuel N.C. *Manichaeism in the Later Roman Empire and Medieval China.* 2nd revised ed. Tübingen: J.C.B. Mohr, 1992.

Lim, Richard. "Unity and Diversity among Western Manichaeans: A Reconsideration of Mani's *sancta ecclesia.*" *Revue des études augustiniennes* 35 (1989): 231–250.

Löhrer, Magnus. *Der Glaubensbegriff des hl. Augustinus in seinen ersten Schriften bis zu den Confessiones.* Einsiedeln: Benziger Verlag, 1955.

MacDonald, Scott. "Augustine's Christian-Platonist Account of Goodness." *The New Scholasticism* 63 (1989): 485–509.

McDonough, B.T. "The Notion of Order in St. Augustine's 'On Free Choice of the Will'." *Irish Theological Quarterly* 46 (1979): 51–55.

McWilliam, Joanne. "Augustine and Ambrose's *sanam fidem.*" In *Charisteria Augustiniana: Josepho Oroz Reta Dicata.* Edited by P. Merino & J.M. Torrecilla. (*Augustinus* 38). Madrid: Ed. Augustinus, 1993, 347–357.

———. "The Cassiciacum Autobiography." In *Studia Patristica* 18/4. Papers presented to the Ninth International Conference on Patristic

Studies held in Oxford 1983. Edited by E.A. Livingstone. Leuven: Peeters Press, 1990, 14–43.

Madec, Goulven. *"Vnde malum?* Le livre I du *de libero arbitrio."* In *"De Libero Arbitrio" di Agostino d'Ippona.* Commented by G. Madec, et al. (Lectio Augustini, 6). Palermo: Ed. Augustinus, 1990, 13–34.

Manferdini, Tina. *L'estetica religiosa in S. Agostino.* (Studi e ricerche, N.S., 16). Bologna: Zanichelli, 1969.

Marafioti, Domenico. "Alle origini del teorema della predestinazione (Simpl. I, 2, 13–22)." In *Congresso internazionale su s. Agostino nel XVI centenario della conversione,* Roma 15–20 settembre 1986, vol. 2. (Studia Ephemeridis Augustinianum, 25). Roma: Institutum Patristicum Augustinianum, 1987, 257–277.

Martinetto, Giovanni. "Les premières réactions augustiniennes de Pélage." *Revue des études augustiniennes* 17 (1971): 83–117.

Mayer, Cornelius, et al., eds. *Augustinus-Lexikon.* Basel: Schwabe, 1986–1994. S.v. "Baptismus paruulorum," by G. Bonner; "Bonum," by N. Fischer; "Concupiscentia," by G. Bonner; "Consuetudo," by A. Zumkeller.

Moon, Albian Anthony. *The De Natura Boni of Saint Augustine: A Translation with an Introduction and Commentary.* (Catholic University of America, Patristic Studies, 88). Washington: The Catholic University of America Press, 1955.

Mutzenbecher, Almut. "Einleitung." In *Sancti Aurelii Augustini De Sermone Domini in Monte libros duos.* (Corpus Christianum, 35). Turnholti: Brepols, 1967, vii–lvii.

Newman, Albert H., trans. "Against the Epistle of Manichaeus called Fundamental." In *A Selected Library of the Nicene and Post-Nicene Fathers of the Christian Church.* Edited by P. Schaff. Vol. 4: *St. Augustin: The Writings against the Manichaeans and against the Donatists.* 1887; reprint, Grand Rapids: Eerdmans, 1983, 125–150.

Nikkel, David H. "St. Augustine on the Goodness of Creaturely Existence." *The Duke Divinity School Review* 43 (1978): 181–187.

O'Connell, Robert J. "The *De Genesi contra Manichaeos* and the Origin of the Soul." *Revue des études augustiniennes* 39 (1993): 129–141.

———. "*De libero arbitrio* I: Stoicism Revisited." *Augustinian Studies* 1 (1970): 49–68.

O'Donnell, James J. *Augustine: Confessions*. 3 vols. Oxford: Clarendon Press, 1992.

O'Meara, John Joseph. *The Young Augustine*. London: Longmans Green, 1954.

Ort, L.J.R. *Mani: A Religio-historical Description of his Personality*. (Dissertationes ad Historiam Religionum Pertinentes, 1). Leiden: E.J. Brill, 1967.

Pegon, J. "Notes complémentaires au *De vera religione*." In *Oeuvres de saint Augustin*. Vol. 8: *La foi chrétienne: De vera religione, De utilitate credendi, De fide rerum quae non videntur, De fide et operibus*. (Bibliothèque augustinienne, 1re série: Opuscules). Paris: Desclée de Brouwer, 1951, 465–499.

Pelikan, Jaroslav. *The Christian Tradition: A History of the Development of Doctrine*. Vol. 1: *The Emergence of the Catholic Tradition (100–600)*. Chicago: The University of Chicago Press, 1971.

Pellegrino, Michele. *Les Confessions de saint Augustin: Guide de lecture*. Paris: Éditions Alsatia, 1960.

Perler, Othmar. *Les voyages de saint Augustin*. Paris: Études Augustiniennes, 1969.

Pincherle, Alberto. *La formazione theologica di sant' Agostino*. Roma: Edizioni italiane, 1947.

———. "Romani 5, 12–13 in s. Agostino." *Studi e materiali di storia delle religioni* 37 (1966): 279–280.

Pizzolato, Luigi Franco. "Il *modus* nel primo Agostino." In *La langue latine, langue de la philosophie*. (Collection de l'Ecole Française Rome, 161). Rome: 1992, 245–261.

———. "Il *De beata vita* o la possibile felicità nel tempo." In *L'opera letteraria di Aogostino tra Cassiciacum e Milano*. Agostino nelle terre di Ambrogio (1–4 ottobre 1986). Edited by G. Reale, et al. Palermo: Edizioni Augustinus, 1987, 31–112.

Portalié, Eugène. "Augustin (saint)." In *Dictionnaire de théologie catholique*. Directed by A. Vacant & E. Mangenot, vol. 4. Paris: Letouzey et Ané, 1903, cols. 2263–2472.

Postma, Elize Baudin Jacques. *Augustinus De Beata Vita*. Amsterdam: H.J. Paris, 1946.

Prendiville, John G. "The Development of the Idea of Habit in the Thought of Saint Augustine." *Traditio* 28 (1972): 29–99.

Ranson, Guy H. "Augustine's Account of the Nature and Origin of Moral Evil." *Review and Expositor: A Baptist Theological Journal* 50 (1953): 309–322.

Rief, Josef. *Der Ordobegriff des jungen Augustinus*. (Abhandlungen zur Moraltheologie, 2). Paderborn: F. Schöningh, 1962.

Ries, Julien. "Notes de lecture du *Contra Epistulam Fundamenti* d'Augustin: à la lumière de quelques documents manichéens." *Augustinianum* 35 (1995): 537–548.

Rigby, Paul. *Original Sin in Augustine's "Confessions"*. Ottawa: University of Ottawa Press, 1987.

Rist, John. "Augustine on Free Will and Predestination." *Journal of Theological Studies* N.S. 20 (1969): 420–447.

———. "Plotinus and Augustine on Evil." In *Plotino e il Neoplatonismo in Oriente e in Occidente*. Convegno internazionale, Roma, 5–9 ottobre 1970. (Problemi attuali di scienza e di cultura, 198). Roma: Accademia Nazionale dei Lincei, 1974, 495–508.

Rivière, J. "Note à *De fide et symbolo.*" In *Oeuvres de saint Augustin.* Vol. 9: *Exposés généraux de la foi: De fide et symbolo, Enchiridion.* 2nd ed. (Bibliothèque augustinienne, 1re série: Opuscules). Paris: Études Augustiniennes, 1988, 66.

Roche, W.J. "Measure, Number and Weight in Saint Augustine," *The New Scholasticism* 15 (1941): 350–376.

Roland-Gosselin, B. "Notes complémentaires aux *De moribus ecclesiae catholicae et de moribus manichaeorum.*" In *Oeuvres de saint Augustin.* Vol. 1: *La morale chrétienne: De moribus ecclesiae catholicae et de moribus manichaeorum, De agone christiano, De natura boni.* (Bibliothèque augustinienne, 1re série: Opuscules). Paris: Desclée de Brouwer, 1949, 513–523.

Rondet, Henri. "La prédestination augustinienne: Genèse d'une doctrine." *Sciences ecclésiastiques* 18 (1966): 229–251.

Salas Martínez, Jesús María. "La maravillosa y misteriosa bondad de Dios hacia el hombre según San Augustín especialmente en sus escritos contra el Pelagianismo y Semipelagianismo." Diss., Fac. Theol. Pontificiae Universitatis Gregorianae, Romae, 1964.

Sfameni Gasparro, Giulia.. "Natura e origine del male: alle radici dell'incontro e del confronto di Agostino con la gnosi manichea." In *Il mistero del male e la libertà possibile.* Lettura dei Dialoghi di Agostino (Studia Ephemeridis Augustinianum, 45). Roma: Institutum Patristicum Augustinianum, 1994, 7–55.

Shimmyo, Theodore T. "Free Will in St. Augustine's Doctrine of Predestination." *Patristic and Byzantine Review* 6 (1987): 136–145.

Slater, Peter. "Goodness as Order and Harmony in Augustine." In *Augustine: From Rhetor to Theologian.* Edited by J. McWilliam, et al. Waterloo, ON: Wilfrid Laurier University Press, 1992, 151–159.

Solignac, Amié. "Introduction et Notes." In *Oeuvres de saint Augustin.* Vol. 14: *Les Confessions: Livres VIII–XIII.* (Bibliothèque augustinienne, 2e série: Dieu et son oeuvre). Paris: Desclée de Brouwer, 1962.

———. "Réminiscences plotiniennes et porphyriennes dans le début du *De ordine* de saint Augustin." *Archives de philosophie* 20 (1957): 446–465.

Stark, Judith Chelius. "The Pauline Influence on Augustine's Notion of the Will." *Vigiliae Christianae* 43 (1989): 345–361.

Svoboda, Karel. *L'esthétique de saint Augustin et ses sources.* Brno: A. Pisa, 1933.

TeSelle, Eugene. *Augustine the Theologian.* London: Burns & Oates, 1970.

Teske, Roland J. "*Homo Spiritualis* in St. Augustine's *De Genesi contra Manichaeos.*" In *Studia Patristica* 22. Papers presented to the Tenth International Conference on Patristic Studies held in Oxford 1987. Edited by E.A. Livingstone. Leuven: Peeters Press, 1989, 351–355.

———. "St. Augustine's View of the Original Human Condition in *De Genesi contra Manichaeos.*" *Augustinian Studies* 22 (1991): 141–155.

Testard, Maurice. *Saint Augustin et Cicéron.* Paris: Études augustiniennes, 1958. (2 vols. in 1).

Thesaurus Linguae Latinae. Editus auctoritate et consilio academiarum quinque Germanicarum Berolensis, Gottingensis, Lipsiensis, Monacensis, Vidobonensis. Vol. 4. Lipsiae: B.G. Teubneri, 1906–1909.

Torchia, N. Joseph. "The Significance of *Ordo* in St. Augustine's Moral Theory." In *Collectanea Augustiniana: Augustine, Presbyter Factus Sum.* Papers originally presented at a conference at Marquette University, Nov. 1990. Edited by J.T. Lienhard, E.C. Muller & R.J. Teske. New York: Peter Lang, 1993, 263–276.

Uña Juárez, Augustín. "*Pulchritudinis leges*: Interioridad y orden en el ejemplarismo estético de san Agustín." *La Ciudad Dios* 208 (1998): 849–882.

————. "San Agustín ante la belleza: Claves de interpretación." *Religión y cultura* 42 (1995): 577–595.

Van der Lof, L.J. "Mani as the Danger from Persia in the Roman Empire." *Augustiniana* 24 (1974): 75–84.

————. "Der numidische Manichäismus im vierten Jahrhundert." In *Studia Patristica* 8. Papers presented to the Fourth International Conference on Patristic Studies held at Christ Church, Oxford, 1963. Edited by F.L. Cross. (Texte und Untersuchungen zur Geschichte der altchristlichen Literatur, 93). Berlin: Akademie-Verlag, 1966, 118–129.

Van Fleteren, Frederick. "Augustine's *De vera religione*: A New Approach." *Augustinianum* 16 (1976): 475–497.

————. "The Cassiciacum Dialogues and Augustine's Ascents at Milan." *Mediaevalia* 4 (1978): 59–82.

Van Oort, Johannes. "Augustin und der Manichäismus." *Zeitschrift für Religions- und Geistesgeschichte* 46 (1994): 126–142.

————. "Augustine and Mani on *Concupiscentia Sexualis*." In *Augustiniana Traiectina*. Communications présentées au colloque international d'Utrecht, 13–14 novembre 1986. Edited by J. Den Boeft & J. Van Oort. Paris: Études augustiniennes, 1987, 137–152.

————. "Augustine on Sexual Concupiscence and Original Sin." In *Studia Patristica* 22. Papers presented to the Tenth International Conference on Patristic Studies held in Oxford 1987. Edited by E.A. Livingstone. Leuven: Peeters Press, 1989, 382–386.

Vanneste, Alfred. "Saint Paul et la doctrine augustinienne du péché originel." In *Studiorum Paulinorum*. Congressus Internationalis Catholicus, 1961, Romae, vol. 2. (Analecta Biblica, 18). Romae: E Pontificio Instituto Biblico, 1963, 513–522.

Vannier, Marie-Anne. "Manichéisme et pensée augustinienne de la création." In *Collectanea Augustiniana: Augustine, Second Founder of the Faith.* Edited by J.C. Schnaubelt & F. Van Fleteren. New York: Peter Lang, 1990, 421–431.

Wenning, Gregor. "Der Einfluß des Manichäismus und des Ambrosius auf die Hermeneutik Augustins." *Revue des études augustiniennes* 36 (1990): 80–90.

Wetzel, James. "The Recovery of Free Agency in the Theology of St. Augustine." *Harvard Theological Review* 80 (1987): 101–125.

Wohlfarth, Karl Anton. *Der metaphysische Ansatz bei Augustinus.* (Monographien zur philosophischen Forschung, 60). Meisenheim am Glan: Anton Hain, 1969.

Zarb, Seraphinus M. *Chronologia Operum S. Augustini: Secundum Ordinem Retractationum Digesta cum Appendice de Operibus in Retractationibus non Recensitis.* Romae: Angelicum, 1934.

INDEX

abstraction, 24, 25
Academics, the, 32
Acta habita cum Felice, 13
Ad Simplicianum, 3, 61, 82, 83–86
Adam, 70, 72, 77
   in Manichaean myth, 41
allegorical interpretation, 43, 44, 63
Ambrose, 90, 91
angels, 48, 85, 86, 87. *See also* spiritual
   beings; Devil, the
animal flesh, 55
anti-Manichaean controversy, 7–9, 15
   debate, 8, 13, 17, 39, 52, 53, 59, 74,
     90
Apostle Paul, 7, 53, 55, 56, 57, 58, 72,
   74, 77, 78, 79
aptum, 24, 26, 33, 37, 39, 64, 68
Aristotle, 24
ascent, 22–26, 70, 73, 77
asceticism, 11
astrology, 5
Atlas, 66
Augustine
   conversion of, 32–33, 41, 91
   Manichaean auditor, 5, 22, 29, 32
   Manichaean influence, 1, 24, 32, 50,
     54, 55, 56, 59, 71
   Manichaean sojourn, 5–6, 22
   self-understanding, 86
authority and reason, 36, 69–70

beatitude, 37, 69
Beautiful, the, 19–20, 21, 23, 26, 32,
   33, 34, 37, 38, 39, 40, 42, 46, 54,
   62, 89
beauty, 3, 18, 19, 20, 21, 23, 24, 25,
   32, 33, 37, 38, 39, 61, 62, 63, 67,
   68, 69, 70, 71, 75. *See also species*;
   forma

and philocaly, 33–34
incorruptible, 18, 19, 30, 38
nature of, 23, 25, 26, 35
sensible, 33, 34
temporal, 18
blindness, spiritual, 82. *See also*
   ignorance

calling, 78
   divine, 3, 46, 61, 78, 83, 84, 86
   effectual, 85
   selective, 81, 83
carnality, 7, 42, 43, 45, 47, 48, 49, 50,
   53, 58, 73, 74, 75, 77, 80, 86
Carthage, 6
Cassiciacum retreat, 73
Catholic Church, 5, 7–9
Cicero, 25, 35, 37–38, 68
commixture of good and evil, 16, 63,
   65–67, 71, 72, 89
concupiscentia, 3, 16, 21, 42, 53–59,
   75, 77, 79, 82, 83, 87, 89, 90, 91.
   See also pleasure, sweetness of
   sexual overtone, 54, 56, 57
Confessiones, 2, 15, 86–87
congruence, 67, 71
consent, 53, 75
consubstantiality, 11, 15–16
consuetudo, 3, 42–53, 55, 57–58, 59,
   69, 73, 74, 75, 77, 79, 80, 83, 87,
   89, 90, 91
contemplation, 24, 25–26, 37–39, 50,
   69, 89
Contra Academicos, 32, 33
Contra epistulam fundamenti, 14, 17,
   18
Contra Faustum, 85, 86
Contra Fortunatum, 52, 58, 74
Contra litteras Petiliani, 13

Patristic Studies

This is a series of monographs designed to provide access to research at the cutting-edge of current Patristic Studies. Particular attention will be given to the development of Christian theology during the first five centuries of the Church and to the different types of Biblical interpretation which the Fathers used. Each study will engage with modern discussion of the theme being treated, but will also break new ground in original textual research. In exceptional cases, a volume may consist of the critical edition of a text, with notes and references, as well as translation. Revised doctoral dissertations may also be published, though the main focus of the series will be on more mature research and reflection. Each volume will be about 250–300 pages (100,000–120,000 words) long, with a full bibliography and index.

Inquiries and manuscripts should be directed to:

> Peter Lang Publishing
> Acquisitions Department
> 516 N. Charles Street, 2nd Floor
> Baltimore, MD 21201

To order other books in this series, please contact our Customer Service Department at:

> (800) 770-LANG (within the U.S.)
> (212) 647-7706 (outside the U.S.)
> (212) 647-7707 FAX

or browse online by series at:

> www.peterlang.com